"In *Dreaming with God*, Sarah Be  of dance—a dance between you ar while following His lead. With tl she gives every woman's heart the Because dreaming means hopin; and every day, with our eyes fixed firmly on Christ as we the beauty of dependence on Him, with each and every step."

—Denise J. Hughes, author of *Deeper Waters*; editorial coordinator for (in)courage by DaySpring

"We all want to follow our dreams, but the question is, how do we get there? Sarah Beth Marr, in her own unique style, brings us to a place of trust and leaning on the Lord rather than simply on ourselves to pursue our dreams. As a ballerina, Sarah not only followed her dreams but also learned to rely on God as her source of strength and hope. Now she shares with us her practical insights to help us settle into a rhythm of grace. You will love her honesty and openness as she leads us to a deeper love for our heavenly Father in *Dreaming with God*."

—Karol Ladd, author of *The Power of a Positive Woman*

"In this inspiring journey, Sarah Beth Marr grabs God's hand and dances into her heartfelt dream. She gathers up inborn talents and, with work and prayer, transforms into a ballerina. Sarah grows into God's purpose and passion for her. But this book isn't just about Sarah. By telling her story—the ups, downs, questions, and perplexities—she encourages readers to pursue their unique paths too. With grace, delight, empathy, and Scripture, Sarah weaves in gentle advice for anyone who craves fulfillment by dreaming with God. If you're seeking purpose and meaning, don't miss this book."

—Judith Couchman, author of *Designing a Woman's Life* and *The Art of Faith*

"As a former dancer, Sarah Beth Marr's debut book, *Dreaming With God*, sang to parts of my soul that have laid dormant. The imagery takes me back to the days at the barre, pointe shoes laced, the pianist waiting for the teacher's direction to start up the music one more time. Sarah calls the reader to the life of a dancer, ready to work and move with the music in dreaming with God. When the music and muscles are working together as they should, we make something beautiful—and soar. It turns out this book spoke to many dormant parts of my soul, those dreams waiting to be uncovered by God's music."

—Alexandra Kuykendall, author of *Loving My Actual Life;* cohost of *The Open Door Sisterhood* podcast

"The Spirit of God is untamed and free, and following Him is never a formula. It's a dance. But all too often we domesticate God's wild and holy moves, and our dreams grow small as a result. In her book *Dreaming with God*, former professional dancer Sarah Beth Marr invites us back into step with our perfect Dance Partner, who leads us in the life we were created for."

—Sharon Hodde Miller, author of *Free of Me: Why Life Is Better When It's Not about You*

"*Dreaming with God* provides wings for your dreams, as Sarah Beth Marr opens your eyes to the beautiful metaphor of dancing by following God's lead. Sharing from her journey as a professional ballet dancer, Sarah Beth gently weaves together personal stories and Scripture, all with the knowledgeable guidance of a caring dance instructor. After just one chapter, I was holding my head higher, paying attention to my posture, and becoming aware of my steps—both literally and figuratively! This book is practical, encouraging, and spiritually uplifting. Readers will love being drawn into the drama and excitement of their dreams. In these pages you will find that following God's lead in the pursuit of those dreams will result in a life-dance that's a bouquet of grace and beauty."

—Rachel Anne Ridge, author of *Flash, the Homeless Donkey Who Taught Me about Life, Faith, and Second Chances*; speaker; and artist

"*Dreaming with God* is a wonderful read, helping us to realize we are not alone on our journeys through life. I definitely have felt stress in my life trying to decide if what I was pursuing was going to work out for me or if I was on the right path. *Dreaming with God* encourages us to see what God has planned for us and demonstrates how His plan may not always be what we think we want, but in the end it is the best plan for us. This book brings ease to the soul and mind."

—Betsy McBride, former principal with Texas Ballet Theater and current artist with American Ballet Theater

"I am grateful that I got to experience this beautifully written book! *Dreaming with God* was a true retreat for my soul. Sarah Beth Marr's authentic point of view invites you to discover God's desire for you to dream with Him. In the truth Sarah Beth expresses in her thoughtful words, I was flooded with encouragement to embrace all He has designed for me to be. Don't miss this book! Grab a warm cup of coffee and soak in these words of encouragement!"

—Katie Norris, founder of Fotolanthropy & Fotostrap; producer of two award-winning documentaries, *Travis: A Soldier's Story* and *The Luckiest Man*

dreaming
with GOD

○ ○

A Bold Call to Step Out
and Follow God's Lead

SARAH BETH MARR

BakerBooks

a division of Baker Publishing Group
Grand Rapids, Michigan

Published by Baker Books
a division of Baker Publishing Group
PO Box 6287, Grand Rapids, MI 49516-6287
www.bakerbooks.com

Printed in the United States of America

Library of Congress Cataloging-in-Publication Data
Names: Marr, Sarah Beth, 1979– author.
Title: Dreaming with God : a bold call to step out and follow God's lead / Sarah
    Beth Marr.
Description: Grand Rapids : Baker Books, 2018. | Includes bibliographical
    references.
Identifiers: LCCN 2017036765 | ISBN 9780801072994 (pbk.)
Subjects: LCSH: Dreams—Religious aspects—Christianity. | Christian women—
    Religious life. | Marr, Sarah Beth, 1979- | Ballet—Miscellanea.
Classification: LCC BR115.D74 M354 2018 | DDC 248.8/43—dc23
LC record available at https://lccn.loc.gov/2017036765

The author is represented by The Steve Laube Agency, Phoenix, AZ. (www.stevelaube.com)

18 19 20 21 22 23 24   7 6 5 4 3 2 1

To the readers
May God spark a light in your heart and
begin a dance in your soul.
Thinking of you makes my heart dance.

Contents

Contents

Introduction

T his book was born out of my search for real, true peace, joy, and contentment in my dream chasing and my daily life. Dance is the language that I know. From the time I was nine years old, ballet captivated my heart. You don't have to be a ballet dancer or know anything about ballet to read this book! My hope is that whether or not you are a dancer, you will enjoy the tidbits about the ballet world and about how, in so many ways, dancing is a beautiful metaphor for our walk with God. This dreaming journey is really *your* dreaming journey. You will hear about my story, but my prayer is that you will find God in a deeper way in *your* story. You see, the sweet thing is, each of us has our own unique dances with the Lord. Your unique journey with the Lord in discovering the dreams He has purposed for you is your dreaming dance.

My background is in professional ballet. I penned my way through the years of dancing professionally, never once thinking I would ever share a word I wrote. I wrote because writing helped me seek God and process what He was teaching me. And through some hoops and hurdles and my own dreaming dance with God, here this ballet of words rests in your hands.

I remember so clearly the day I tentatively mentioned to my husband, Brian, my desire to write books. Back then I simply wanted to encourage ballet dancers in their walk with the Lord, something I was desperately looking for when I was a young professional dancer. I wanted to hear from someone who understood the ballet world. This dream began to swell in my heart, and I finally whispered it to God, then to Brian. Thankfully, Brian did not think I was crazy! He believed in this little dream. And it became a dance. It became a dance of learning, trusting, waiting, and growing, and I am so thankful it found its way to your heart. I am praying for your heart that as you journey through these pages, you discover dreaming with God is the sweetest dance.

One thing I love about the ballet studio is that when you enter, you can leave everything else outside the doors and just go in and dance. To get into the zone of the music and the movement is to find a little relief from stress and life. I pray this book is like a little getaway for your heart and a retreat for your soul. I hope you can set aside some things for a while, set down some stress, and zone in on God's heart for you in your own dreaming journey. On that note, I want you to know that this book is meant for your own scribbles. I want you to make it your own—mark it up and dog-ear the pages. At the end of each chapter, you will have room to answer some reflection questions and extra space to record your thoughts. My hope is that this book becomes a journal of your own dance with the Lord.

I'm so excited to send you off on your journey with the Lord. He truly is calling *you* to dream with Him. His grace is the place where you can lay down your striving, your discontentment, your desires, and your dreams and trade them in for His strength, His peace, and His direction. The pathway to this place of grace—this place of deep joy and contentment with who you are and to Whom you belong—is surrender. This surrendering of your life and your dreams is a daily dance of surrendering every detail and every dream—every day. I pray your soul begins this life-changing dance today.

1

○ ○

Searching for God
in Your Dreaming Journey

You lifted me out of the depths . . . you turned my
wailing into dancing.

Psalm 30:1, 11

I was born a dreamer; it's in my blood. My sweet parents always
encouraged me to follow what God had put in my heart. The
first big dream I remember having as a little girl was to go to the
1996 Summer Olympics as a gymnast. I studied the competitions
of the elite gymnasts that my dad recorded for me on our VCR. I
memorized and mimicked their every move and position. I worked
tirelessly to perfect my skills by spending hours upon hours at the
gym. The gym became a second home. It seemed like I had chalk
from the uneven bars all over me at all times. I loved it. Gymnastics
became a passion—and a dream. After a few years, I started growing and became a tall, lanky gymnast who had lost all control over

her long limbs. My growth spurt completely threw off my timing, and I quickly became discouraged. Add in the pain of tendonitis and the fear of some of the big tricks I was learning, and this dream slowly started to lose its appeal. With tears, I let this dream go. A short time later, I wanted to be an Olympic horse jockey and compete in equestrian riding and jumping. Once again, that dream went downhill as I realized I was not brave enough for that.

Falling in Love with a Dream

Around the time I let go of my Olympic dreams is when I started taking ballet classes. It wasn't love at first sight. It was more of a slow realization that ballet was a good fit for me. My height did not hold me back, and ballet wasn't nearly as frightening as gymnastics because, for the most part, we stayed fairly close to the ground! My ballet teacher recalls that I came to my first ballet class with no tights (which is pretty much a no-no in the ballet world) and with chalk covering my legs from being at the gym. I was stiff, but she took notice of my strength. I was turned in, but she saw I had the flexibility to turn out. I was also intense and serious, which she knew was needed to be a dancer. And I was disciplined from all my gymnastics training. The music and the movement grabbed my heart. And my dancing journey began.

As I became more and more involved in the ballet world, performing onstage and playing a role captured my heart. It began to dawn on me that I enjoyed not just that dancing was physically challenging; I was delighted to dive into different characters. Although I was falling in love with ballet, at the time I had no idea it would become my profession. In fact, I didn't even know dancing could be a profession. I will never forget the first time I saw, in person, a performance with real, professional ballet dancers. It was *The Nutcracker* and the guest artists were two dancers from New York City's American Ballet Theater. Paloma Herrera danced the role

12

of the Sugar Plum Fairy. She was amazing. She took my breath away. She had the strength, power, and perfect lines of a gymnast but the artistry, softness, and radiance of a ballet dancer. She was this perfect blend of beauty, grace, strength, and athleticism. For the first time, a light bulb went off in my heart. *Paloma is doing this for a living. This is her job. She is getting paid to do this.* And a seed was planted in me.

After getting more serious about my training, I ventured into auditioning for summer programs and eventually for ballet companies. Dancing professionally became a reality for me, and I'm so incredibly grateful. It never felt like a "job," and I often couldn't believe I was getting paid to do what I loved. Becoming a professional ballerina was no easy journey, and it became more of a spiritual one than a physical one as I learned to lean in to my relationship with the Lord for guidance, strength, and help. My dancing journey also propelled me onto a path of dreaming in other areas of my life.

When Dreams Pull Your Heart in Different Directions

After my dream of becoming a professional ballet dancer came true, other dreams would strike a chord in my heart . . . dreams of finding my husband, starting a family, living in a house, being a stay-at-home mom, passing on my faith to my children, writing. I often felt my dreams conflicted with one another. Many times I put pen to paper, asking God how Brian, babies, and ballet fit together. There were geographical, physical, and emotional obstacles. My dreams and my heart's desires seemed to pull me in different directions at times.

Dreaming is one of God's tools to draw us close to Him.

But dreaming, I now realize, is one of God's tools to draw us close to Him.

One night a couple of years ago, Brian surprised me by arranging a sitter to watch our boys while we went on a date to hear an interview with a ballerina I had admired for years. By this point, I was living my dreams of being a professional ballerina as well as a wife and a mom. My hope at the time was to keep dancing for several more years, so I was ready to soak in any words of wisdom she had to help me in my dancing career. I wanted to know the secrets to her success.

We got all dressed up, fancier than my typical jeans and flip-flops, and headed downtown to hear what this famous and extremely talented dancer had to say. In the car, my heart leapt with excitement as I anticipated her message. I was also extra giddy that my sweet husband would surprise me with a night out. We found two vacant seats in an intimate and completely packed theater. The audience represented all walks of life, all ages, from little ballerinas to older couples.

The lights dimmed and the famous ballerina stepped out onto the stage. We all went bananas with cheers and applause. She settled into her chair across from the man who would be interviewing her and told her incredible story of trials and triumphs. Then she offered up the microphone for a question and answer time. Too many hands to count popped up from the audience. The questions that came up the most were something to the effect of "What got you through all those hard times?" and "What would be your message to people who are following their dreams?" Her answers echoed with the overarching theme of "pull yourself up, work as hard as you possibly can, be determined to succeed, and you can make your dreams come true."

As she spoke, I felt a heaviness, an uneasiness, because my heart wanted to hear God somewhere in the equation of following my dreams. Hers was the message I was used to hearing in the ballet world, but I wondered where God fit into it. I don't believe she said anything wrong, and clearly she had worked incredibly hard to get to where she was. Talk about a life of sacrifice, discipline, and hard work. I knew those things were part of following my dreams. Ballet was not an easy profession. The bloody blisters on my toes, aching pains in my ankles, and sore muscles all over my body were part of a normal workday. Sweat, tears, hard work, and the quest for perfection were part of the job. But was that it? The evening seemed to stir up all my dreaming questions again.

I know part of my heaviness was because I'm a thinker, a feeler, and a gal who had fallen in love with Jesus. I longed to know how He fit into this dreaming dance. That ballerina's message seemed like the popular message of our current culture—dream big, follow your dreams, be determined, go for it, make things happen, push yourself. But as a believer, I started wondering, *What's the message for women who desire to follow God and follow their dreams?* I was suddenly very aware that the world's message and God's message seemed to be two different paths.

As Brian and I waited in a line to meet the famous ballerina and get her autograph, I tried to shove down all my dreaming thoughts and questions. The uncomfortable angst of figuring out how to flesh out my walk with Jesus in regard to the dreams of my heart gnawed at me. As we drove to one of our favorite restaurants just north of downtown Dallas, I truthfully felt confused (hence the deep thinker in me). *Do I want to follow my dreams? Am I following the right ones? Does Jesus care about my dreams? Do I have to make my dreams and my life happen all on my own by working really hard?* These thoughts lingered in my head and my heart over fajitas and guacamole. *What did God have to say?*

Your Dreaming Journey

Sometimes I wish I could go with the flow a bit more and just be okay with the simple idea that "You can make your dreams come

15

true." I wish I could rest in that and joyfully go about chasing those dreams down. But I've always sensed a red flag in my heart regarding that message, which doesn't completely resonate with me. It felt like the world's message conflicted with my faith in the Lord. The world seemed to shout, *chase, strive, and make it happen*, but Scripture echoed *trust God, be still, and wait on Him*. The two messages felt at odds with each other. That evening is one of the many times I have heard that type of message and have felt that little red flag go up. My dreaming journey involved learning to dream *with* God.

I'm so excited to bring this dreaming message to your heart. I invite you to explore with me to see if there is another way to follow your dreams. I'm not a famous ballerina. Not even close. I'm a wife. I'm a mom. I like to write. And I danced.

○ ○ ○ ○ ○

Dreaming with God is the sweetest dance.

○ ○ ○ ○ ○

That's me, and if we could sit together over coffee or tea and discuss this dreaming dance, maybe you would ask, "What's the key to following the dreams God has for you?" I would smile inside, because while I don't know all the answers, I have so felt the same question. In that moment, I would grab a refill of coffee, pull out my stacks of journals, push them all toward you, and say something like this: "Dreaming with God is the sweetest dance. I don't have all the answers, but here's what I've learned from seeking the Lord in my dreaming questions."

So I'm giving you all I've got. My hope is that you're able to unravel your heart from the world's rhythms and find a new rhythm of prayer and surrender in your dreaming journey by dreaming with Him. A new level of grace, joy, peace, and rest in *His* plans for you by dreaming *with* Him. These plans may be different from your own. And that can be hard to hear in a "dream big" kind of world. But I believe God has called us to dream with Him, and when we do, our hearts will begin to dance in a new way.

When we accept God's invitation to dream with Him, we're relieved of the pressure to hold our lives and our dreams together on our own. We instead find a sweet spot of living out the dreams God created us for. In that choice—and it's a daily one—Christ takes the lead, and we find jewels along our life paths. We're going to dig up those jewels throughout these pages. The biggest impact we can make on the world is to be close to Jesus, and following our dreams with the Lord becomes the road map to a deeper relationship with Him.

> God wants in on our dreaming journeys.

The world will continue to encourage us to follow our dreams on our own, to dream big and make things happen for ourselves. And, truthfully, I don't think anything is wrong with that! I just believe God wants in on the plan. God wants in on our dreaming journeys. He offers a message that's whispered, not shouted. A narrow road. A quiet path. An unpopular and countercultural way of dreaming. His plans may not involve fame, fortune, and bright lights, but could they be more satisfying and sweeter than we could imagine?

Prayer, Scripture, and Reflection
for Your Dreaming Heart

Lord, I bring You all my questions and confusion about the messages I have heard. I invite You to open my heart to see You in this dreaming dance.

"You lifted me out of the depths . . . you turned my wailing into dancing." Psalm 30:1, 11

"Taste and see that the LORD is good; blessed is the one who takes refuge in him." Psalm 34:8

"The LORD is close to the brokenhearted and saves those who are crushed in spirit." Psalm 34:18

"Why, my soul, are you downcast? Why so disturbed within me? Put your hope in God, for I will yet praise him, my Savior and my God." Psalm 42:11

1. What are your dreams and desires?

2. In regard to following your dreams, what message from the world do you hear most often?

3. How have the messages of the world affected the way you go about following your dreams?

4. What dreams do you feel discouraged about?

2

Spotting the Truth
about Who You Are

For we are God's handiwork, created in Christ Jesus
to do good works, which God prepared in advance
for us to do.

Ephesians 2:10

I believe the place to start dreaming with God is in Scripture. A ballet dancer keeps her eyes focused on one object when she is turning. Dancers, you know this—you breathe it and practically do it in your sleep. A dancer focuses on one object, turns, and whips her head around quickly to bring her focus right back to that same spot. This spotting prevents dizziness and keeps her balanced. And so, in this same fashion, we as daughters of Christ can spot the truth of what Scripture says about who we are to God, who He is, and what He has to say about our dreaming hearts.

Made and Loved by God

Before you set out on your dreaming journey, God invites you to see yourself as He sees you. He handpicked your personality traits, your character qualities, and even your quirks. He drizzled in some unique talents, abilities, and skills and sprinkled in emotions and compassion to stir things up a bit. What you see as weaknesses, He uses as strengths. He made you just the way He wanted. You're not a rough-draft version of yourself. He doesn't want you to try to be like everybody else. He wants you to be *you*! Dreaming with God is becoming the *you* He had in mind when He made you.

Scripture tells us in Psalm 139:13–14 that each of us was made by God, intricately fashioned and designed by Him. Many of us have heard this truth before, but over time, the messages we hear and see from the world drown out God's truth. In a sense, we lose our spot, our focus on who God says we are. If I could just look you in the eyes for a moment, I would love to pour some truth from Scripture right into your heart. Be warned, this is about to get really mushy . . .

> *He knows you better than anyone.* "You have searched me, LORD, and you know me." Psalm 139:1
>
> *He knows your thoughts.* "You perceive my thoughts from afar." Psalm 139:2
>
> *You are beautiful to Him.* "You are altogether beautiful, my darling; there is no flaw in you." Song of Songs 4:7
>
> *He sees you as forgiven, cleansed of your sins.* "Though your sins are like scarlet, they shall be as white as snow; though they are red as crimson, they shall be like wool." Isaiah 1:18

> Dreaming with God is becoming the you He had in mind when He made you.

22

He is always with you. "Do not fear, for I am with you." Isaiah 41:10

He created you for His glory. "Everyone who is called by my name, whom I created for my glory, whom I formed and made." Isaiah 43:7

He made you and formed you. "He who made you, who formed you in the womb, and who will help you." Isaiah 44:2

He thought you up before the beginning of time. "Before I formed you in the womb I knew you, before you were born I set you apart." Jeremiah 1:5

He loves you. "I have loved you with an everlasting love; I have drawn you with unfailing kindness." Jeremiah 31:3

He delights in you and sings over you. "The LORD your God is with you, the Mighty Warrior who saves. He will take great delight in you; in his love he will no longer rebuke you, but will rejoice over you with singing." Zephaniah 3:17

He knows the number of hairs on your head. "And even the very hairs of your head are all numbered." Matthew 10:30

You are His daughter. "I will be a Father to you, and you will be my sons and daughters, says the Lord Almighty." 2 Corinthians 6:18

You are His child. "So in Christ Jesus you are all children of God through faith." Galatians 3:26

He cares about every detail of your life. "Cast all your anxiety on him because he cares for you." 1 Peter 5:7

Below is a section of Psalm 139 I really want you to soak in as a message to your heart. Insert your name in these verses, or any of the verses above, and be encouraged. I also changed the *I*'s to *she* below to help us see that this is a message for each of God's daughters:

O Lord, you have searched Sarah.

You know when she sits and when she rises; you perceive
her thoughts from afar.

You discern her going out and her lying down; you are familiar with all her ways.

Before a word is on her tongue you know it completely, O
Lord.

You hem her in—behind and before; you have laid your
hand upon her.

Such knowledge is too wonderful for her, too lofty for her
to attain.

Where can she go from your Spirit? Where can she flee
from your presence?

If she goes up to the heavens, you are there; if she makes
her bed in the depths, you are there.

If she rises on the wings of the dawn, if she settles on the
far side of the sea,

even there your hand will guide her, your right hand will
hold her fast.

If she says, "Surely the darkness will hide me and the light
become night around me,"

even the darkness will not be dark to you; the night will
shine like the day, for darkness is as light to you.

For you created Sarah's inmost being; you knit her together in her mother's womb.

She praises you for she is fearfully and wonderfully made;
your works are wonderful, she knows that full well.

Her frame was not hidden from you when she was made
in the secret place, when she was woven together in the
depths of the earth.

Your eyes saw her unformed body; all the days ordained
for her were written in your book before one of them
came to be.

Many of us have heard these familiar words, but somewhere along life's path, we lost sight of them or maybe even stopped believing them. As I drive my boys to elementary school, I love asking them the same old question, and they always give me the same answer. "What's the first verse that pops into your head as you head into school today?" I ask. With giggles and smiles, they shout, "God knows how many hairs on your head!" (their version of Matt. 10:30). And we laugh together, and it never gets old. It's a silly little thing we do, but I long for the message to sink into their hearts that God knows them and made them each so special. I want them to be amazed by our big God who is all-powerful but also personal. And as they tumble out of the car, the verse catches my heart by surprise, reminding me that this truth is not just for little ones—my grown-up heart needs to remember it too.

All the days ordained for her were written in your book before one of them came to be.

You may have heard it said a thousand times, but are you living like you know you are made and loved by God? You are wired by the God of the universe for a specific purpose. He thought you up before you were even conceived. To be thought about, dreamed up, and created by God . . . let that sink in for a moment. He created the way you smile, the way your eyes light up when you laugh, the tilt of your head when you are making a decision, and the carriage of your walk. He picked out the color of your hair and formed the muscles in your body. He carefully tailored your personality to match your unique calling. He sprinkled in love, joy, and delight and mixed it up with His expertise and gentle care. He made your toes, your nose, and your eyelashes. And He delights over you. You are one of His masterpieces. It sounds so amazing when we stop to really think about the wonder of it all, but when life gets full, we forget Who we belong to. We forget we are made in the image of God.

I always love hearing the story my mom tells of when I was born. She cried tears of joy when she found out I was a girl. She held me on her shoulder her whole hospital stay. That makes me feel so special. Now I love telling my boys the stories of when they were born. What astonishes me as a mom is how different each of them looked when they were born. I assumed they would all look alike for some reason. My first son, Camp, was born with hair as dark as mine and lots of it! The nurse was able to comb

> He wants us to feel confident in who He made us to be and at peace with the way He made us.

over his hair from birth, and he immediately had a traditional, freshly combed boy cut right from the start. So precious. My second son, Cooper, was born big and strong, and his hair was light-colored like his daddy's. Cooper had his own special look and personality. Then when my third son, Colt, came along, the first thing we said when he entered the world a couple weeks early was, "He's so tiny!" And to top it off, he had blue eyes, unlike his brown-eyed brothers. God is incredibly creative to give each of them their own unique look and personality. I could write a book about each of them and how I would never want to change anything about them.

I'm sure that's how God wants us to feel about ourselves, although not in a haughty or prideful way, but in an awestruck, confident way. He wants us to feel confident in who He made us to be and at peace with the way He made us.

He wants us to see the goodness of the way He thought us up. My favorite little jewel in Psalm 139 is hiding in verse 14: "I know that full well." These words challenge us to know—to really, really know—we are fearfully and wonderfully made. I think I lived many years of my life knowing this but not understanding or believing it "full well." My hope is that together we can start to grasp the sweetness of this truth in a deeper way. When we spot the truth about who we are as God's daughters, we will see our own very individual, incredibly handcrafted, one-of-a-kind beauty, and that will completely impact our dreaming journeys.

One wonderful thing about understanding how God sees us is that it points to how amazing He is. That He knows us so personally and loves us so deeply speaks of His majesty and greatness. That He breathes life into us points to His unfathomable power. Psalm 139 is not just a self-esteem pick-me-up; it's a beautiful reflection of worship to our powerful and sovereign God. Seeing Him as Creator leaves us in awe of Him—and that's a beautiful place to begin our dreaming journeys.

Gifted and Wired on Purpose

In addition to your physical body and creatively designed appearance, God also intricately shaped and crafted your heart, with all its quirks, desires, feelings, emotions, dreams, gifts, talents, abilities, callings, and personality. We tend to be hard on ourselves for being a certain way. I get goose bumps during Christmas commercials, I cry through worship songs at church, and I get giddy over coffee with pumpkin spice creamer. Sometimes I step through piqué arabesque when I'm walking from the den to the hallway, I could sit on my back porch for hours with my journal and pen, and my favorite place on earth is at home with all my boys. Pots of flowers speak to my soul and long walks are my go-to source for

> He is going to use the shape of your heart to shape the world around you.

stress relief. Sitting by my mom's fireplace, coffee cup in hand, is a place I love to be. Pedicures with my sister are a must—not so much for the pedicures but for the time with her. *Dancing with the Stars* gives me chills and browsing bookstores, well, be still, my heart. That's just the short list!

All the little things that seem insignificant—even pointless— are God's touch of creativity in each of us. The things that give us joy, make our hearts go pitter-patter, and provide us a boost in our day are the very things given to us by God to bless us and steer our hearts toward His dreams for us. What makes you giddy? Are you outgoing or more introverted? What makes your heart dance? What are your likes and dislikes? I encourage you to start a list of the little things that make you *you* and spot the truth that God made you this way! And you know what else? The little things you do and say, the little things that make you who you are and separate you from the crowd—they make God's heart dance. They may even make Him laugh. Your uniqueness, quirks, personality, and gifts make you stand out, and they are needed in this world. God shaped your heart the way He did to make an impact on the world and to move you to embrace all He designed you to be. He is going to use the shape of your heart to shape the world around you.

Our dreaming journeys with God begin when we see that the way He made us actually points to His dreams for us.

Scripture is our strong foundation for the dreaming ahead. For a ballet dancer, doing exercises at the barre every day is sort of like brushing your teeth every day. It's something you've got to do. Barre is a dancer's foundation for all her dancing and performing. Her technique is refined and strengthened at the barre. The exercises she repeats over and over again protect her from injury, warm up her body properly, and prepare her for her load of rehearsals and performances. The dancing all begins at the barre. In the same way, our journeys

○ ○ ○ ○ ○

The dancing all begins at the barre. In the same way, our journeys of dreaming with God begin in Scripture.

○ ○ ○ ○ ○

of dreaming with God begin in Scripture. When we spot the truth that out of His great love for us, He created, wired, and shaped us with special purposes in mind, our sweet dances of dreaming with God really begin. As we dance through our journeys together, may we continuously spot the foundational truth about who we really are—loved and unique daughters of Christ—and who He is—our Creator and Savior.

Prayer, Scripture, and Reflection
for Your Dreaming Heart

Lord, help me spot the truth about who You made me to be. Thank You for lovingly creating me for Your glory and for specific purposes You have in mind for me. Thank You for the gift of Scripture, and may it always be the foundation for my dreaming heart.

_____

_____

_____

_____

"Your word is a lamp for my feet, a light on my path." Psalm 119:105

"The unfolding of your words gives light; it gives understanding to the simple." Psalm 119:130

"For we are God's handiwork, created in Christ Jesus to do good works, which God prepared in advance for us to do." Ephesians 2:10

_____

_____

_____

_____

1. How has God personally gifted and wired you?

_____

_____

_____

·_____

2. How does spotting truth about who you are affect you as you dream?

_____

_____

_____

_____

3. What negative thoughts about who you are need to go?

_____

_____

_____

_____

4. As you reflect on God's creativity, how does it affect your view of Him?

_____

_____

_____

_____

3

○ ○

Soaking in God's Heart for You

"For I know the plans I have for you," declares the
LORD, "plans to prosper you and not to harm you,
plans to give you hope and a future."

Jeremiah 29:11

One of the dilemmas of my heart in regard to this dreaming
dance has been my wondering if God even wants me to
"dream big." Many times, when my dreams seemed impossible,
I felt like dreaming big was kind of a selfish and disheartening
pursuit. As a little girl, I had tons of dreams, but as I became a
grown-up, responsibilities, reality, and practicality seemed to sup-
press my dreaming heart. I wondered if dreaming was even good
for me. But God has shown me that He desires for us to dream
with Him because it actually makes our hearts dance, helps us
know Him better, and points others to Him. God wants us to
allow Him to guide us to the dreams He has for us, which come

in all shapes and sizes. Dreaming then becomes a divine pursuit instead of a selfish one.

In this chapter, I want you simply to soak in God's desires for you in regard to your dreaming journey.

Dreaming Makes Our Hearts Dance

In the fall of 2015, I walked my oldest son, Camp, to his very first football practice. It wasn't even an official practice, more of a pre-practice to get in shape for the real practices. He was only nine years old. My little man jumped out of bed early with excitement. He was dressed and ready to go way before I was. He had been waiting for his turn to play football—and suddenly it was here. My mama heart saw a little man with big dreams and a big heart, and his joy and excitement reminded me of what God does in us through the dreams of our hearts.

> Dreams are boosts of grace, joy, and delight that give our often weary hearts little tastes of heaven.

God wants us to know that dreams make our hearts dance. Dreams give us wings. Dreams are boosts of grace, joy, and delight that give our often weary hearts little tastes of heaven.

Dreams push us to God's heart because they are improbable, seemingly impossible, and sometimes over our heads, and all we can do is hold them up to our Maker. Dreams seem to chase us, then pull us back, then knock us down, and then inspire us. Dreams make our hearts beat a little faster. Dreams make our souls soar a little higher.

My son, in all his joy that morning, reminded me that dreaming is good for our hearts. Even for a busy mama, even for a dancer whose body was feeling too old for professional ballet that morning, and even for a writer who at the time felt her writing dreams were on hold. Dreaming does something in us. Something heavenly.

Something divine. I believe God wants us to dream with Him because dreaming makes us giddy, for lack of a better term.

When Mary's Heart Danced

God's dream for Mary made her heart dance. In Luke 1, the angel approached Mary and said, "Greetings, you who are highly favored! The Lord is with you" (v. 28). The angel's words greatly troubled Mary, and she wondered what kind of greeting this was. Then the angel said to her, "Do not be afraid, Mary; you have found favor with God. You will conceive and give birth to a son, and you are to call him Jesus" (vv. 30–31). The angel went into deeper detail about God's dream for this ordinary gal and ended with this: "For nothing will be impossible with God" (v. 37 ESV). After the shock wore off and Mary received some encouragement from Elizabeth, Mary's heart began to dance with a new song.

> My soul glorifies the Lord and my spirit rejoices in God
>   my Savior,
> for he has been mindful of the humble state of his servant.
> From now on all generations will call me blessed, for the
>   Mighty One has done great things for me—holy is his
>   name.
> His mercy extends to those who fear him, from generation
>   to generation.
> He has performed mighty deeds with his arm . . . . has
>   lifted up the humble.
> He has filled the hungry with good things. (vv. 46–53)

As Mary allowed herself to believe God was serious about this dream for her, her heart exploded in joy and praise to Him. She didn't know how the dream would work out, she didn't know for certain it would turn out, and she didn't have a detailed plan to see the dream through. But God had given her a dream. And it made her heart dance.

Permission to Dream

God desires for us to give ourselves permission to dream because dreaming keeps our hearts dancing. When we dream, we live full of hope, possibilities, and purpose, and living this way has a beautiful effect on our hearts and the hearts of those around us. Many times throughout motherhood I wanted to know whether it was okay for me to keep dreaming. I would have loved for someone to have said, "Yes, keep dreaming" or "No, now's not the time." Maybe you've felt this way, but I want you to know that God wants us to keep dreaming in every season. He wants us to dream even when the logistics of our dreams don't seem possible. But in the dreaming, He longs for us to keep Him in the lead.

> In the dreaming, He longs for us to keep Him in the lead.

He also wants us to see a deeper purpose for our dreaming. After all, dreaming is not just about us. Dreaming is a path to getting to know Him and pointing others to Him. Just as the dream God gave Mary was not just for her, although it deeply blessed her, God has dreams for each of us that reach farther than we think. God's dreams for us are actually pathways to His heart, as well as to others' hearts. God wants us to allow Him to guide us into the dreams He has for us.

The Emotions That Surface When We Dream

Following, pursuing, and thinking about our dreams can feel heavy because dreams are intensely personal. They hold our innermost desires, our passionate emotions, along with our deepest fears and insecurities. An abundance of emotion is tied to our dreams. And we all have experienced how a dream, big or small, can even break our hearts.

Many times throughout the years, my fragile emotions surfaced and I couldn't put a name on my dream. I felt restless, hungry for purpose and passion, but at the same time, I was powered by my "mama bear" instincts. I longed to keep life simple so I could focus on raising my sons with my husband. I flitted around different possible ideas in my heart, thinking that when I found the "right" one, the angst would go away and I could get busy living my dream. My ideas ranged from starting a ballet company in Dallas to starting my own leotard line to beginning a cross-training program for dancers to teaching ballet. I had all sorts of ideas and desires, and I was antsy to find my thing. I had fun with these ideas one day and then got mad at them for feeling so impossible and distracting on other days. Deep down I was grieving the loss of the ballet company I had danced with for so long. They were having financial troubles, so I wasn't getting to dance as much as I was used to. I was trying not to be sad about not dancing, but deep inside, that was my dream. All these other ideas felt like backup dreams. My heart was tender from emotion, raw from disappointment, and a little embarrassed that I felt clueless as to what the answer was. I wondered if it was time to turn off the dreaming switch of my heart because all this dreaming felt too hard on my heart.

One afternoon, the artistic directors from the ballet studio I grew up dancing at swung by my house to borrow something. I worked really hard to put a smile on my face and a bounce in my step, not wanting to hint to them that I felt a little lost. They asked how things were going with the ballet company, and I let them know it was not looking too good. Most dancers would've picked up their lives and found another company in a different city to dance for. However, Brian and I did not want to move because our little family felt established in Dallas, so I felt as if dancing professionally was slowly slipping from my life. I tried to hide my emotion and disappointment from them. What I really wanted to do was ask them for wisdom, but I kept my heart tucked away inside.

Not long after their visit, one of them called me, and it turns out she had read me like a book. She saw the hurt, angst, disappointment, and emotion in my eyes that day. She didn't know all the details of what I was feeling, but she reminded me that God was at work in my life—that He had planted many little seeds in my heart and they were just waiting to grow, sprout, and blossom. She didn't have an exact answer for me, but she encouraged me to keep seeking God. In that moment, I felt God was sending me a little divine reminder that He wanted me to keep dreaming and that all those tiny desires sprouting up were divine jewels of direction He wanted me to pay attention to.

In the following months, new desires seemed to bud—ones that surprised me—such as the desire to write books. This desire felt as though it came out of nowhere, but at the same time it felt like a puzzle piece that I had been looking for had fallen into place.

It seemed that little hints of this writing dream had been planted along my journey. As I looked to God in that season, He faithfully steered my heart.

> God is at work in your life, guiding you to the dreams He has for you.

Like a runner passing a baton in a relay race, sweet daughter of Christ, I pass on this gem of encouragement to you: God is at work in *your* life, guiding you to the dreams He has for you.

He has planted all these little seeds in *your* heart, and they are just waiting to grow, sprout, and blossom. He wants you to keep dreaming, and He uses all your desires and dreams to get you to the ones He made you for.

His dreams are a perfect fit for you. It's as if He's the choreographer and you're the dancer. Because He knows you so well and created you to be different from anyone else in the universe, He knows the dance in life that's perfect for you. Just as a choreographer draws on a dancer's strengths and individuality to create the most beautiful dance for her, God longs to put into place dreams that He choreographed just for you before you even entered this world. Instead of spending a lifetime chasing dreams that are a better fit for someone else, He longs for you to embrace a better dance: your dance. The path to your own unique dance is often hidden in the desires of your heart.

God Uses the Desires of Your Heart

I think we all struggle at times to know whether listening to the desires of our hearts is a good or a bad thing. My sweet mom has been the person in my life who has taught me to dream with God by tuning in to Him through the desires of my heart. Here is one of my favorite Bible verses she introduced to me back when I was a young lady on the edge of adulthood: "Take delight in the LORD, and he will give you the desires of your heart" (Ps. 37:4). I love this verse because it gives us permission to listen to the desires of our hearts, but there is a little twist to the verse: "Take delight in the Lord." Delighting in God and Him giving us the desires of our hearts can sometimes feel like two different things. Mom taught me that when we delight in God first and foremost—in a sense, make our dreaming about knowing Him—He shapes our desires. And that's when we can listen to the desires of our hearts because they are in tune with God's heart. When we are tuned in to God's heart regarding the dreams He has for us, He delights to give them to us.

Desires will ebb and flow throughout our dreaming journeys. We can put every desire in God's arms, and He will guide us to the dreams He has preplanned for us. God is the Dream-Planter. He loves to plant little seeds of dreams in our hearts that He will use to lead us through life, give us great joy, guide us in living out the gifts He has put in us, and help us make an impact on the world around us.

As I look back over my own dreaming dance, sometimes I laugh at how a little desire would seem to pop up out of nowhere and shift something in my dreaming path. One example is when I showed up late to a MOPS (Mothers of Preschoolers) meeting. It was the first one of the year, and I really didn't know anybody. As I rushed through the door, this lady, who I later found out was the speaker coordinator, came running up to me and with excitement and enthusiasm hugged me and nearly shouted, "Are you our speaker for today?" The speaker for that day was also late and also had long, brown hair. Eyes wide, I assured her I was not the speaker for the day, and somewhere deep inside this little conversation with myself took place: *I could never, ever do that. Please don't make me! How scary. What would I even have to say? But that does sound kind of fun. But who am I? I could never, ever do that.* The speaker finally did show up, and I went home that day and scribbled those little thoughts to God in one of my journals. I gave Him that teeny, tiny desire even though I didn't know whether it was from Him. A couple years later, I began speaking to MOPS groups. Now speaking to groups of women has become a little dream that makes my heart dance. God took a small desire and used it to steer me in the direction of His plans for me. I think it's incredibly beautiful how He does that.

This dreaming dance requires us to constantly check in with God to see if our little desires or big passions are something He wants us to pay attention to. Sometimes our desires and God's desires don't match up, and that's okay, but we must be willing to allow God to shift our desires if He sees fit. That is part of dreaming with Him. He will keep our hearts on course. We just need to take to God the desires, dreams, and ideas that sprout up in our hearts. Typically, they will feel like crazy ideas. Some may never even come to fruition. The desire that comes over me to be a country music singer is a great desire, but y'all, singing is not one of my strengths. Deciding if that desire in particular is one God wants me to pursue or not is very clear to me because I do not have the vocals to match the desire. But other desires can be trickier to decipher. Sometimes I bring a desire of my heart to God, and I cannot tell how He feels about it. That's when I wish He would send me an email! I have brought other desires to God as well, and it's almost as if the moment I bring them to Him and say them out loud or scribble them into a journal, I'm suddenly very aware that they're not something I should pursue. But when we give ourselves permission to express a desire out loud to God, to bring it to Him, He takes it and clarifies His purposes for us.

○ ○ ○ ○ ○

He will keep our hearts on course.

○ ○ ○ ○ ○

Dreaming in All Shapes and Sizes

God's heart for all of us is that we would see that dreams come in all shapes and sizes. Some of us are going to have dreams that involve a stage, lights, and an audience, and some of us are going to have dreams that no one sees. Some of us have wild, impossible dreams. Some of us love the quieter kind. Some of us dream of the spotlight, while some of us want to steer clear of it! For some of us, our dreams revolve around our homes. For some of us, our dreams reach into faraway places. Also, we will have multiple dreams throughout our dreaming dances. We have big dreams and everyday dreams. Glamorous dreams and simple dreams. Every dream and desire is valuable in God's eyes. His heart for us is to dream in all kinds of ways.

He wants us to dream big . . . and small and in all kinds of shapes and sizes. God wants us to dream with Him so that our hearts dance with joy and purpose, so that we get to know Him in deeper ways and point others to Him.

41

As we talked about in the previous chapter, remember this: He divinely designed your heart, mind, and soul to fit specific callings. And He uses the twists and turns of your heart shape to draw you into all He created you to be. Oh, how He wants you to be all He designed you to be. He does not want you to miss out on the dreams He has planned for you.

Prayer, Scripture, and Reflection
for Your Dreaming Heart

Lord, make me a dreamer, because dreaming draws me closer to You. Help me listen to the desires of my heart, but at the same time, let me take each one to You. Help me decipher which desires are Your desires for my life and which are my own. Help me be willing to let You shape and mold the desires of my heart into the dreams You have for my life.

"May the favor of the Lord our God rest on us; establish the work of our hands for us—yes, establish the work of our hands." Psalm 90:17

"When anxiety was great within me, your consolation brought me joy." Psalm 94:19

"'For I know the plans I have for you,' declares the Lord, 'plans to prosper you and not to harm you, plans to give you hope and a future.'" Jeremiah 29:11

_____

_____

_____

1. Do you allow yourself to dream or have you turned off the dreaming switch in your heart?

_____

_____

_____

_____

2. What are some of your big dreams? What are some of your small dreams?

_____

_____

_____

_____

3. Which desires of your heart do you need to bring to God? Are there any you feel Him asking you to let go of?

_____

_____

_____

_____

4. What emotions surface when you think about the dreams of your heart or the ones you consider giving yourself permission to dream?

_____

_____

_____

5. Describe a time you let go of a dream and it turned out for good.

_____

_____

_____

6. As you give yourself permission to dream, what effect does it have on your heart?

_____

_____

_____

4

○ ○

Surrendering to God's Lead

Yet you, LORD, are our Father. We are the clay, you are
the potter; we are all the work of your hand.

Isaiah 64:8

My favorite part of being a ballet dancer was when the opportunity arose to work with a partner. There's nothing
like performing a pas de deux where you get to be lifted high into
the air, be held just perfectly on balance on the tip of your pointe
shoe during a pirouette, and have someone out onstage with you.
The experience is indescribable, and it's a beautiful team effort.
When dancing with a partner, someone has to take the lead—and
it's always the male dancer. Occasionally I unintentionally tried
to take the lead out of sheer panic or fear or because it felt easier.
Doing so created tension because we were not dancing in sync. We
were off the music or just not connecting. Our movement became
restrictive and choppy. It just didn't flow. As difficult as it is, the
female dancer has to let go of leading and allow the male dancer

45

to lead in order for their movement to flow beautifully. For her, a *letting go* has to happen.

As we give ourselves permission to dream and follow after the desires God places in our hearts, there is a letting go that has to happen in our hearts. We too must let go of leading. God is trying to lead us to His dreams for us, but we tend to fight His guidance because it's our natural inclination to do so. But He longs for us to let go and surrender to His lead.

> He longs for us to let go and surrender to His lead.

Taking Your Grip off Your Dreams

Instead of striving with an "I am determined to make this happen" attitude, God longs for us to dream with a surrendered heart, saying, "Whatever You want, God." The first option—striving on our own—puts our dreams on our own two shoulders. The outcome rests on us. We go to extremes to conquer our dreams, causing wear and tear on our hearts as we strive, stress, and strategize to make them happen. We try to manipulate things, we take the reins of our own lives, and we leave God out. The problem with holding on too tightly to our dreams is that they can become a stronghold in our lives. Then when those dreams don't come true, we are emotionally wrecked because that dream had become our very life.

The other option is realizing that dreaming requires a surrendered heart. It means taking our grip off our dreams so God has room to work. Surrendering protects our hearts when our dreams don't go as planned because we have grounded our lives in the Dream-Giver rather than the dream. In surrendering, we put our dreams in God's capable hands. Through the process, we learn there are no other hands we would rather lay our dreams in than His. Surrendering means we let God be in control and leave the outcome up to Him.

A Dance of Trust

Once we've taken that step of surrendering our dreams, we begin a dance of trust. Some days we will truly feel at peace, trusting that God is at work behind the scenes. But other days we will lose our footing, seemingly unable to get our emotions in line with surrendering. Those days feel cloudy, as if our faith in God is fogged up by questions and doubt. We tend to be hard on ourselves on those days because we think we should be able to trust God and be at peace, but remember: it's a dance. Swaying back and forth between trust and doubt is how our faith grows. Getting to that place of true peace can mean two steps of faith forward and one seed of doubt backward. But as we sway through this dance of growing in our faith, God brings us to a place where we deeply believe that His will and His ways are best. Then we can take our grip off our dreams and trust His lead. Surrendering our dreams means surrendering not only the outcome of our dreaming journeys but also the road map to getting there. It means trusting Him with every detour, delay, and U-turn along the way. When we don't have a choke hold on our dreams, our lives are free to flow in the beautiful grace of God's direction.

○ ○ ○ ○ ○

When we don't have a choke hold on our dreams, our lives are free to flow in the beautiful grace of God's direction.

○ ○ ○ ○ ○

Remaining Flexible

Another aspect of surrendering to His lead is remaining flexible. A ballet dancer spends a lot of time stretching her body—splits and hamstring and calf stretches. She stretches to protect her muscles from injury and to enable her to move her body from one extreme angle and position to another. Surrendering to God's lead means remaining flexible with regard to God's ways and God's timing as He stretches our hearts to trust His lead.

When I receive emails from my blog readers, particularly from young, aspiring ballet dancers (and often their caring parents), their questions usually revolve around the same topic: They really want their dreams of dancing professionally to come true, so they are doing everything in their power to make it happen—taking extra ballet classes and private lessons, losing weight in extreme ways to fit the ballerina body mold, growing competitive with their fellow dancers. Their hearts are set on their dreams, and they are fixated on pursuing them. But they email me in frustration because obstacles are popping up and their dreams are just not coming true. They ask me, "Why would God lay a dream on my heart that's looking like it is not going to happen?" I've been right there in their pointe shoes, feeling those same feelings.

The decision to dance or not to dance after the birth of each of my babies was never a simple or easy decision. I often wished God would send me an email to make the answer ultra clear! Navigating this decision felt like this dance of tug-of-war within my heart, but God always faithfully guided me.

After my second son, Cooper, was born, I felt conflicted about whether to return to ballet. Navigating that decision was an emotional process for me as a young mom because while I loved dancing, I loved being a mom too. My heart felt torn in two different directions. I didn't know if it was possible to juggle dancing well with two kiddos. After seeking the Lord about it over a period of nearly a year, I truly felt like He gave me the green light to dance! I was about thirty years old and dancing for a smaller company, so I thought it was time to really, really go for it—to work as hard as I could, dance big, be committed, and dance my heart out. A dancer's career can be quite short compared to other occupations. As I entered my thirties, I knew my dancing clock was ticking, so I was relieved to finally make the decision and get back to dancing. I had a cross-training plan in place so I could be at my best physically for the strenuous rehearsals and performances ahead. All gung ho, I was ready to do whatever it took to reach my goal of becoming the best dancer I could possibly be. I was ready!

After finally feeling at peace about being a mom *and* a dancer, I entered the ballet studio for the first day of our new season. Everyone in the ballet company was excited to start rehearsals and there was no denying the energy in the room as we warmed up at the barre in class that day. A fresh season gave everyone a fresh start, and I could tell we were all ready to dance. My heart was beating with joy, and I enjoyed class a little more than usual because I was simply so excited. But after class something out of the ordinary happened. Typically after class we would take a short five-minute break and then return to the studio for rehearsal. But something was off that day, because instead of starting rehearsal, we were asked to gather together and sit down. A meeting like this was a rarity in our company. I can remember how quiet the room grew as we each slipped on our warm-ups and gathered around. We were gently given the news that the company was having serious financial problems. Our season would be cut down to only a few *Nutcracker* shows rather than our whole season, and the future of the company looked quite grim. The artistic team basically told us to go home for two months until *Nutcracker* rehearsals began and to not count on the company being around much longer after that. I was one of the veterans who had been dancing with the company for years, but a handful of others were beginning their very first day as professional dancers. For all of us, this news was devastating.

Like I mentioned earlier, Brian and I had no plans of moving to a new city to follow my dancing dream. My heart sank. Tears flowed. My dream was heading down the drain. Just a short time earlier I had been convinced that God had prepared my heart to really go for it in my dancing. In the moments after hearing that disappointing news, though, an unexpected peace washed over me. I felt this peaceful shift of the winds of my life changing. I felt a giving up, a letting go, an *Okay, God, You lead; I can't figure this out.* In my angst, I felt carried. God's presence seemed closer as I let go of leading my life, and my boys' company over the next few weeks felt like a soothing balm to my dreaming heart.

I had to let that dream of dancing full-time go, and it was harder than I can describe. God softened the blow when, two months later, I found out I was expecting my third son, and I actually danced in *The Nutcracker* while pregnant. It was quite an adventure battling morning sickness while dancing the role of the Dew Drop Fairy, but it was a special time of learning to see that God's plans are greater than my own. My heart was broken from one dream crashing, but God swept me up off my feet with a better plan. I learned to ride the waves of His grace. I learned that I don't want to get off the ship of His lead, His plans, and His dreams for my life, because even though I cannot always see it, His dreams for me will bring more joy than my own plans ever could. So I often encourage young aspiring dancers to be flexible, to be willing to dance or not to dance. It's in that place of flexibility in our dream chasing that God meets us with His divine plans for our lives.

> It's in that place of flexibility in our dream chasing that God meets us with His divine plans for our lives.

Letting God Take the Lead

We have to be willing to let go of steering our lives and let God lead. He wants in on our dreams. I cannot tell you whether your dreams will come true, but I can tell you that if you invite Jesus into the process and look to Him first and foremost, leaning on Him, He will guide you to the dreams you were made for.

Sometimes I feel the itch to steer my own life. My fleshly desires tempt me to take the lead. I see a dream in front of me, and I just *want that* dream. But things aren't that simple. I have to remind myself that, yes, nothing is impossible with God but also that *His* plans for me are for my good. I'm often confronted with the reality that sometimes the dreams I see in front of me—my ideas—aren't for my good. Oh, they're appealing in the world's eyes, but something deep inside me is throwing out a red flag. I choose to believe that it's the Spirit steering. Often, I want to ignore Him, but when I remember He has my very best interests in mind, I begin to loosen my grip.

At times I have really had my heart set on a specific dream. The angst of the wanting often left me empty-hearted. When our hearts get attached to a dream, we need to bring it to the One who wants to steer our lives. Otherwise, we dream and we chase and we manipulate our lives in ways that are harmful to our dreaming hearts. Sweet one, God knows what is best for you. He knows the path you need to be on and the one you should avoid. I know how disheartening it can feel when it seems that your dreams and God's dreams for you don't match up. It can feel like a death to self and to your own dreaming heart to lay down those dreams at His feet. But the most amazing transaction happens when we let our ideals and dreams go and trade them in for His plans for our lives. Peace. Know today that God's dreams for you are for your very best and for His glory. When you finally lay down your dreams is when He picks you up with His beautiful plans for your life. Will you lay it all down today?

When I was dancing, I learned that although at times I couldn't understand or see it, my ballet director really did have my best interests in mind, and he could see the whole picture of what the upcoming performance was supposed to look like. I would go about my dancing and rehearsing thinking I was doing pretty good, but he would stop me and gently point out things in my movement that were a little off. It was hard to take at times, but I noticed that when I embraced his vision, trusting he could see the dance as a whole, well, things went smoother. My movements looked cleaner and felt better. When I followed his lead, I was free to reach my potential in that particular role.

○ ○ ○ ○ ○

When you finally lay down your dreams is when He picks you up with His beautiful plans for your life.

○ ○ ○ ○ ○

God sees things we don't see. God sees the whole of your life with eyes of love, vision, and purpose. When we pull away from Him, we cannot step into His best for us. However, when we lean in to His vision, we move toward His plans for our lives. As we prioritize Him—His ways, His thoughts, His truth over our ways, our thoughts, and our opinions—we get to dance the adventure He designed for us.

Knowing When to Let Go of a Dream

Sometimes we keep chasing a dream that's just not meant to be, which we figure out only as we seek Christ. But there is beauty in knowing when to let go of a dream. And when we do, we can find peace in knowing that although that dream's not meant for us, the dreaming, the bringing it to God's hands, the praying over it (which we're going to talk about in the upcoming chapters) . . . all had a purpose. God used it to shape us, teach us, and bring us closer to the plans He had for us all along.

One dream I had to let go of was dancing in a big, prestigious ballet company like American Ballet Theater or Pacific Northwest Ballet. In the ballet world, there are big companies and smaller companies. The big ones have more dancers, more money, more extravagant productions, bigger audiences, and more performances.

The smaller companies have fewer dancers, less money, fewer extravagant productions, smaller audiences, and fewer performances. Some dancers prefer bigger companies, while others like the size and feel of a smaller company. Finding a job as a professional ballerina is a difficult endeavor either way because companies can only have so many dancers. They are looking for a particular set of technical, physical, and professional standards. For a while, I had my heart set on those bigger companies. I auditioned for these companies but knew that being hired was a total long shot because I did not train in their schools. Most big ballet companies only hire dancers that have trained at their school for many years. In one rejection letter, I was told that while I exhibited beautiful legs, feet, and lines, the odds of making it into the company were not in my favor because I hadn't trained in their school. They recommended that I search elsewhere for a dancing position. In another letter, I was told I was not a strong enough dancer. And another company simply told me there were no openings. The sting of rejection hurt.

I knew it was time to move on from my dream of dancing in a larger company. I could have chosen to keep prying my way in. I could have chosen to find a way, any way, in. I could have gone on a crash diet to better fit the ballerina mold or begged for a second chance. I could have gotten mad at everyone around me because I was frustrated about the entire situation. But none of those tactics would have worked. Instead, I had to come to terms with the truth dawning in my heart that even though I couldn't see what God was doing, His plans for my life were better than the plans I had dreamed up for myself. As I surrendered to God's lead, my dreaming heart seemed to settle into its home back in the sails of God's lead.

It chokes me up to think about His plan, which I knew nothing about at the time, because it included becoming a wife to Brian and a mama to my three precious boys and dancing for a smaller company that would allow me the flexibility to be with my sons

as much as possible. His plans also included this book you're
reading right now, which I honestly don't think I would have felt
the need to write had my dreams worked out the way
I thought they should have. I would never go back and
change a thing.

*God will
get you
to where
you need
to be.*

So I encourage you to hold your dreams up in trust to
God and surrender to His lead. I know it's scary. I know
that sometimes it's incredibly upsetting when your dream
is not happening. I know it's heartbreaking and confusing
when you have to say goodbye to a dream. And I know
it's frustrating when the road ahead seems unclear. God
sees it all. And He's there for you, guiding you to His good plans
for you. And He will get you there as you let go and let Him lead.
Lean in to Him, dear one, and enjoy the ride. God will get you to
where you need to be.

Prayer, Scripture, and Reflection
for Your Dreaming Heart

*Amazing Lord, help me want to give You the dreams of
my heart. Help me trust Your lead and believe Your plans
for my life are far better than anything I could think up.
And Lord, thank You that dreaming draws me closer to
You. May my dreams make me fully dependent on You as
I seek Your plans and Your heart for my life.*

"Unless the LORD builds the house, the builders labor in vain." Psalm 127:1

"Trust in the LORD with all your heart and lean not on your own understanding; in all your ways submit to him, and he will make your paths straight." Proverbs 3:5–6

"Seek first his kingdom and his righteousness, and all these things will be given to you." Matthew 6:33

1. Does it feel difficult at times to surrender your dreams to God? If so, why?

2. Which dreams seem appealing but deep down you know they aren't God's best for you?

3. Think seriously about your life for a moment. Have you been letting God lead your life or have you been taking the lead?

4. In what way have you attempted to make your dreams come true on your own?

5. What questions about your own dreaming journey could you bring to God today?

6. How do you feel about the thought that God's dreams for your life are better than your plans?

5

Settling into a Rhythm of Grace

Are you tired? Worn out? Burned out on religion?
Come to me. Get away with me and you'll recover
your life. I'll show you how to take a real rest. Walk
with me and work with me—watch how I do it. Learn
the unforced rhythms of grace. I won't lay anything
heavy or ill-fitting on you. Keep company with me and
you'll learn to live freely and lightly.

Matthew 11:28–30 Message

Without the Lord's help, following our dreams can become a frantic chase involving a rhythm of stress and angst as we take things into our own hands, do things our way, and pursue our dreams as if it's all up to us. But when we surrender to God's lead, He invites us into a different rhythm—one led by Him. It doesn't mean we don't work hard, only that we don't have to chase and force our dreams because we are inviting the God of the universe into the process to guide us and lead the way. He takes off the pressure of holding up our dreams on our own and instead guides our hearts through every step of our dreaming journey. As we step into His rhythm of grace, understanding that ultimately He is in control, we no longer have to chase the dream down or frantically force the dream into fruition. Instead, we find a place of keeping company with Jesus in our dreaming journeys—a place of prayer and rest and embracing the season we're in.

Praying through Your Dreaming Journey

One aspect of God's rhythm of grace is prayer. Prayer is the rudder to our dreams. As we pray, God directs and guides, keeping us on the course He has created for us.

When we pray about our dreams, we invite God into our lives—something He longs for. Through prayer, we bring our dreams to the God who turned water into wine, multiplied bread to feed thousands, healed the sick, lame, blind, and deaf, and raised Jesus from the dead. In today's fast-paced, technology-based, insta-everything world, we tend to leave out the miraculous. But God is still working miracles in the world, and He wants to work miracles in the dreams of our hearts.

> o o o o o
>
> As we pray, God directs and guides, keeping us on the course He has created for us.
>
> o o o o o

After I had let go of my dream to dance for a big company, I waited for some direction from God. I was an apprentice at Ballet Austin at the time, and it was nearing the end of the ballet season, which is when decisions are made about hiring new dancers and letting others go. I would have loved to have danced for Ballet Austin as a company member, but I knew there were no openings, or so I thought, at the time. There were ten apprentices, so even if the main company had an opening, my chances were quite slim. Typically, if the main company has no opening, the apprentices are let go so they can search for a position with a different company.

And like I mentioned earlier, finding a dancing job at any size company is quite difficult.

During one of the last rehearsals of that season at Ballet Austin, we were in the middle of rehearsing for *Don Quixote*. I was doing my thing—stretching out my calf muscles, reviewing corrections, steps, and musical cues in my head—when I felt a tap on my shoulder. To my surprise, it was my artistic director. He was the director of the main company, while another director handled the apprentice company. I worked with both very closely in rehearsals, but of course, as a young aspiring ballerina, I was a little intimated by both of them. My dancing career was in their hands in a sense, and so I always wanted to be on my game around them. He asked me to come down to his office on our next five-minute break. My first thought was that I was in trouble for something, but I couldn't imagine what it could be. Per his request, at the next break and with butterflies in my stomach, I headed down the stairwell to his office. My heart was in my throat. As I sat down across from my director, he looked very serious. He mentioned something about me understudying a role because one of the dancers was struggling with an injury. Then he stopped for a moment and called in the director of the apprentice company. She came in with a bit of a smile on her face. They informed me that one of the dancers had decided to hang up her pointe shoes, so they had one opening in the company, and they offered me the position. My jaw literally dropped. I cried and laughed, and then I hugged them both. I think I was jumping up and down too. I really never dreamed that dancing for Ballet Austin's main company was an option for me. I thought either there were no openings, or if one became available, they would not choose me. The competition for a spot was fierce. It was amazing to realize that God had a good plan all along. Ballet Austin was and still is an excellent company, one I feel so grateful to have had the opportunity to dance for. I danced there for a total of five years before Brian and I moved to Dallas, where I continued my dancing career with Ballet Arlington. I will always feel indebted to my directors at both companies for believing in me and giving me the opportunity to dance professionally.

God's plans for me were far better than I could even imagine. And His dreams for you are far better than you can imagine. Looking back, I realize that God wants us to pray and trust Him even when we don't know what the answers should be.

> God wants us to pray and trust Him even when we don't know what the answers should be.

We discover His beautiful plans as we release our desires and dreams in prayer. Sometimes we really want our options to work out the way we want them to work out. Life can feel disappointing in those moments when we don't get our dream job or the good news we were hoping for, and I have had plenty of those moments along my journey. (We are going to talk more about that in the upcoming chapters.) So I encourage you to pray about the dreams of your heart even when you cannot imagine how the situation should turn out. Prayer invites God to work out the details.

But He doesn't want us to pray only about our big, impossible dreams. He wants us to pray about everything—even the tiniest details!

> Do not be anxious about anything, but in every situation, by prayer and petition, with thanksgiving, present your requests to God. And the peace of God, which transcends all understanding, will guard your hearts and your minds in Christ Jesus. (Phil. 4:6–7)

Our relationship with Him grows sweeter as we spend time with Him in prayer. He begins to unfold His dreams for us and move those dreams forward as we settle into a rhythm of prayer. Also, we get to know Him better and experience His peace in a deeper way as we bring Him each burden. He keeps us in His lighter, freer rhythm of grace.

Contentment in Your Current Season

Another aspect of God's rhythm of grace is discovering contentment in our current season. Sometimes we miss the gift of our current season as we are dreaming about future ones.

In 2010, I had just had my third son. I was one busy mama with a baby, an almost two-year-old, and a five-year-old. I was tired. But the thing was, I was tired of feeling so tired. Getting my babies to sleep all night never came easy, so I was living in a fog of sleep deprivation and fatigue.

One day while my older two sons were at preschool, I crawled up into my bed hoping to catch a quick nap while they were taken care of and the baby slept.

> Prayer invites God to work out the details.

In that moment, I felt so frustrated that I couldn't function well enough to do more than take a nap. The night before had actually been a fairly good night for us in regard to sleep, so I was disappointed that I still felt so exhausted. I was in a Bible study group during that season and had told my leader a few weeks before about the dream in my heart to write one day. But in this weary, sleep-deprived moment, I remember thinking there was no way I would ever feel energetic enough to do that.

My leader happened to call me that day as I was settling in for my nap to ask me how I was doing. Tears sprang to my eyes as I expressed to her how I was tired of being tired. It kind of makes me giggle now, but in that moment, my fatigue and exhaustion were totally consuming. I told her that I don't know why I was so tired because the night before had been pretty smooth. In a gentle voice and with great wisdom from being a few seasons ahead of me in motherhood, she reminded me that this tiredness and sleep deprivation were part of a season. She reminded me that I wasn't just tired from the night before—in reality, I hadn't slept consistently in five years! Also, my body had been through a lot in the last five years. We calculated that I had been pregnant for a total of twenty-seven months between my three sons, and I had been nursing for almost two years. Add to that the lack of consistent sleep, and she sweetly diagnosed me as one tired mama deep in the trenches of mothering little ones. She challenged me to let go of my expectations of being super productive or pursuing big dreams during this season and instead encouraged me to be gentle on myself. My heart started to feel a little relief in that moment as I listened to her. Next, she nearly shouted through the phone, "When is your baby going to be four?" We did the math together and again she shouted, this time with such joy and exuberance, "Summer of 2014!" that I was somewhat confused. She told me that when my youngest turned four, I would be sleeping consistently all night, every night (I would have liked to have gotten that in writing), my body would have recovered fully from pregnancy and nursing, and I would have much more time to take care of myself and consider the dreams budding in my heart.

At first I felt even more overwhelmed at the thought that four years seemed like a long time away. But then, as we talked, she helped me realize that 2014 would be a new season. And somehow in that moment, my heart found relief and comfort as I saw these seasons from a new perspective. I hung up the phone and drifted off into a deep sleep. I learned to embrace my current season and enjoy doing the things right in front of me instead of constantly wishing for the next season. The summer of 2014 came, and my Bible study leader was right. We were all sleeping through the night consistently, and I had much more time and margin in my day to dip my toes into my writing dream. I think a delightful thing about God is that He continues to give us dreams throughout all the seasons of our lives. We will always be tempted to skip to the next season or dream, but God longs for us to be fully present in our current season.

During my years of dancing, there was a constant emphasis on our musicality when dancing. It became like second nature for me to dance "with the music," for every step, every movement, and every breath to go with each beat of the music. Learning this vital skill takes years of practice and intentional focus. It doesn't make sense to be "off the music." Dancing off the music would mean falling behind or rushing ahead of the music, as if the dancing does not go with or match the music. When a dancer is off the music, many problems arise. For example, the audience may find the performance difficult to watch because it distracts from the overall flow of the show. It can wreak havoc on a group of dancers—we're talking traffic jams and collisions onstage—who have to be perfectly in tune with each other. It can stir up conflict among the dancers because that one dancer who is off the music becomes the target of bad vibes from the artistic director and causes everyone to have to put in additional rehearsal hours. (And I have so been that dancer off the music, by the way!) It restricts the dancer who is off from dancing freely, with abandon, because being off the music does not make sense to the body or the brain. It frustrates the dancer. But when all the dancers are with the music, something magnificent happens—pure beauty and impressive unison! When a dancer is on her music, not rushing ahead or lingering behind, it's as though the music carries her, freeing her to reach her greatest potential.

In the same way, God is here in this moment and in this season, offering to carry us through it. When we jump ahead mentally to

> We will always be tempted to skip to the next season or dream, but God longs for us to be fully present in our current season.

the next season, we miss out on His beautiful rhythm of grace. Yes, we can still dream with God in our current season, trusting His plans for a future one. But we mustn't neglect today. When we welcome our current season and choose to be in the present moment with God, we're free to enjoy and thrive in our current season, in perfect unison with God's good timing.

Embracing the Process

Another aspect of staying in this rhythm of grace is learning to embrace the process of following a dream with God.

The rehearsal process for ballet was certainly not the highlight of the job for me. I could hardly wait to get to performance day. We all have a tendency to want to see the good, fun part—the result of a dream. But as we learn to embrace the hard part, the journey, and the process, we discover a new level of joy and contentment in our lives. It's in the process that we find God's guiding hand and learn to lean on Him for our every step.

Oftentimes we want overnight success, but the realization of our dreams takes time. All the small steps in our dreaming journeys matter. We easily become discouraged when it feels like a dream is taking forever to come to fruition. The process is where God works in our hearts, hones our skills, directs our hearts, and loves on us. The process is the good stuff of following a dream. It will involve setbacks, highs, lows, frustrations, and breakthroughs. There will be parts of the process that require great patience, hard work, and a full schedule, and there will be slower parts of the process where God teaches us to enjoy the ride.

When we lean in to the process, what we're actually doing is trusting God with our dream. We're trusting His timetable, His way, and His plan. In this trust, we can let go of our tendency to rush things and lean back into a rhythm of rest. Know that dreaming with God is a lifelong process.

Rest from Striving

With God, it is possible to dream and rest at the same time, trusting our dreams to the One who also calls us to a sweet rhythm of rest. This rest is part of His rhythm of grace and is more of a heart check, a knowing that God is in control of our lives so we don't have to live at a chasing, striving, and stressful pace. This is where the sweet spot of dreaming with God is found. While dancing, I was always coached to "push down into the floor," while at the same time "stand tall" as if the tip of my head was going through the ceiling. This vital posture makes a dancer strong, stable, and grounded; it also adds an elegance to her dancing. In the very same way, God invites us to keep dreaming while we embrace the process. He invites us to settle in, nestle down, and push down into the process, while at the same time look to Him as He leads us toward the dreams ahead. So we remain strong, stable, and grounded wherever we are in the process because we are standing tall with our feet planted in contentment and our dreaming hearts secure in His lead.

Another aspect of rest in our dreaming is looking to Jesus for His ways and wisdom. I love how Jesus said, "Get away with me and you'll recover your life. I'll show you how to take a real rest. Walk with me and work with me—watch how I do it" (Matt. 11:28–30 Message). It seems to me that in this verse, Jesus was saying that by getting away with Him, we recover our lives—or in this instance, our dreams. As we walk with Him, work with Him, and partner with Him instead of chasing our dreams on our own, we can simply watch how He does it.

You know that dream in your heart that has been gnawing at you as you read these pages? You can let go of trying to figure out how to make it happen. You can set it down, retreat with Jesus, and look to Him for help. He will show you how to truly rest from the striving. Getting away with Jesus is the most productive thing you can do in living out your dreams.

We really can let go of the chase. We really can let go of trying to make our dreams happen. We really can rest back into a rhythm of grace. Every moment oozes with purpose when we enter into His beautiful rhythm of grace. And here's the sweetest news: settling into this rhythm sets us on His perfect course for us. We can let go of managing, manipulating, and strategizing our lives and instead focus on Him. Because that's where He meets us with dreams and joys we did not see coming. I imagine He can barely contain His excitement as we get to a place of letting go and letting Him lead our dreaming journeys.

> ○ ○ ○ ○ ○
>
> Getting away with Jesus is the most productive thing you can do in living out your dreams.
>
> ○ ○ ○ ○ ○

Writing about this brings up emotions of relief for me. It reminds me that I don't have to do life, mommyhood, marriage, dancing, writing, or dreaming by striving on my own. I don't have to become who God created me to be in my own strength. He takes off the pressure. And when I embrace His graceful pace, I feel the joy bubble up.

Each of us will find unique ways to settle into this rhythm of grace. My all-time favorite way can be summed up in two wonderful words: *porch time* (and maybe one more word: *coffee*). Get me on a porch, birds chirping, sun casting beams through the branches of a redbud tree, flowers looking lovely, Bible open . . . just me, my Bible, a journal, my Lord, and my coffee . . . that's where I find God's rhythm. That's where I get back to Him when I've gotten caught up in the world's pace. That's where I draw near to Him and He gently draws me back into His way of grace.

You know, some of the most beautiful moments of a pas de deux occur when the pair is just standing still. Those moments of little movement, only the subtle gesture of a hand or the look of emotion in their eyes, can be the most impressive. I believe that in this dance of life, those moments when we retreat with Jesus to settle into His rhythm are our most beautiful.

Prayer, Scripture, and Reflection
for Your Dreaming Heart

Lord, thank You for inviting me into Your beautiful rhythm of grace as I dream with You. Show me specifically what steps I can take to settle into Your rhythm. Help me settle into this way of grace so I can find a deeper relationship with You through prayer. I want to embrace the season I am in, take my hands off my dreams, and rest in knowing You have them.

"The LORD will fight for you; you need only to be still." Exodus 14:14

"The LORD is my shepherd, I lack nothing. He makes me lie down in green pastures, he leads me beside quiet waters, he refreshes my soul. He guides me along the right paths for his name's sake." Psalm 23:1–3

"Be still, and know that I am God." Psalm 46:10

"There is a time for everything, and a season for every activity under the heavens." Ecclesiastes 3:1

"In his love and mercy he redeemed them; he lifted them up and carried them all the days of old." Isaiah 63:9

"I am the vine; you are the branches. If you remain in me and I in you, you will bear much fruit; apart from me you can do nothing." John 15:5

1. Which aspect of God's rhythm of grace speaks to your heart the most? Prayer? Seasons? Process? Rest?

2. What are some practical ways you can settle into God's rhythm of grace?

3. What dreams of your heart and details of your everyday life do you desire to bring to God in prayer?

4. What season are you in and how can you sink down into it even more?

_____

_____

_____

5. In what ways do you find yourself tempted to skip to the next season or dream?

_____

_____

_____

6. Where are you in the process of one of the dreams of your heart and how can you fully embrace the process?

_____

_____

_____

7. In what ways can you let go of striving to make your dream happen?

_____

_____

_____

6

○ ○

Securing Your Hope as You Wait on Your Dreams

I wait for the LORD, my whole being waits, and in his word I put my hope.

Psalm 130:5

Once we settle into God's rhythm of grace, we will find that waiting is part of dreaming with God. Waiting for our dreams to unfold is part of the process, and, as I'm sure you know, it can be hard to wait and keep believing that God is at work behind the scenes of our dreams. Sometimes we just need a little heart pep talk in our waiting moments.

The Tension of Waiting

During my own waiting moments, I often found myself stuck. I was stuck in this space of being too anxious to move forward with joy and too preoccupied with angst to embrace contentment. Instead of flourishing while I waited for my dreams to unfold, I often found myself wilting in the waiting. I longed, and still do, to flourish in the waiting from a fixed confidence, knowing God is at work on my behalf. Many times I blurted out all my dreaming/waiting angst in a blubbery mess of tears and emotion to Brian because I felt unable to handle the wait. I wanted to live with peace even when I felt my dreams were on hold or completely impossible.

The tension of hoping and wondering about our dreams can bring us to a state of depletion and take a toll on our dreaming hearts.

I too have felt the weight of my dreams, particularly my dream to write. One morning in 2015, as I crawled out of bed, *tired* felt like the word of the day. Not so much a physical fatigue, but a heart fatigue: weak from wondering and worn from waiting. I knew in my heart I should trust God with my dream to write, but I felt clueless as to how to turn it over to Him and wait well. How do we hand over an intangible dream? How do we release a burden that keeps burdening us? How do we find relief from the angst?

I saw dark circles under my eyes as I began my family's get-ready-for-school routine. I sensed that my dreaming heart was even interfering with sound sleep, so extra coffee seemed like a good idea. I got the boys to school and took a quick shower. I had a speaking engagement to get ready for, so I pushed those dreaming thoughts deep down and tried to focus on making it there on time. I vowed to take a power nap later. Before I headed out, I checked my email hoping for some type of answer to my author dream. Nothing. Maybe tomorrow.

At the speaking engagement, I encouraged a room full of moms to dream with God and let Him lead. But when I walked out, my own heart felt incredibly heavy because it seemed my dreams were on hold, were never going to happen, or were going to take forever. I thought a nap was what I needed. But after getting all cozied in bed, I realized that what I really longed for was soul rest—to let go of my dreams and all the stress I was holding on to in the waiting. I longed for the deep peace of being able to truly trust God with my dreams in the waiting. Instead of a nap, I grabbed my pen and journal and placed my dream of writing in God's hand through my scribbles. With each page of my thoughts that I released to Him, the tension of the wait seemed to ease more and more.

The Sweetness of Waiting

Waiting for a dream to unfold or an answer to finally show up can feel anything but sweet. After waiting and discerning, we finally feel like we know what God has called us to do, and so in faith we do that thing, only to have to wait some more. We tend to want to know God's plans ASAP. We think if we just knew how our dream was going to turn out, then we could live in the wait with peace. But God understands that we wouldn't need Him if we knew the outcome of our dreams.

The final weeks of waiting for Camp, my oldest, to be born, tested my patience. I was pretty uncomfortable physically and so ready to meet this baby. Meeting him was the dream of my heart during that season. I headed to my doctor's visit about a week before he was due, sure that she was going to announce that Camp would be arriving any day now. Instead, she assured me Camp would go all the way to his due date. Awesome. Instead of heading home, I pulled into the frozen yogurt shop, ordered my favorite flavor, white chocolate mousse with Heath bar slivers, and downed it. I was frustrated. I was tired of waiting. I did not handle the waiting well in that moment.

When I got home, I set about rearranging my living room furniture. I don't know why; I just felt the need to rearrange. Later that afternoon, my water broke and Brian and I headed to the hospital. Our sweet Camp was born a week early. God knew all along.

Some days I handle the waiting super well. I typically accomplish a lot while I wait. I organize closets. I fold lots of laundry. I'm intentional with my kiddos. I cook dinner. It helps me to keep moving in the practical things of life as I simply try not to think about the dreams of my heart. And then other days I simply don't handle the waiting well. I get anxious. I worry about the unknown. In these times, I'm tempted to figure things out, make things happen, or get the ball rolling on my own. Doesn't it seem easier sometimes not to wait on God? Doesn't it seem easier to take the matter into our own hands? Doesn't it seem easier to give up on God? That's where I was that day after my speaking engagement and at the frozen yogurt shop before Camp was born. I was fed up with the waiting. But in the heart-to-hearts I have with God about my dreams being seemingly on hold, in His faithful way, He reminds me that He is with me in the wait. All His truth pours in and it is as if He whispers to my soul: "Daughter, You are mine. Daughter, I'm at work. Daughter, I have it all under control. You don't have to plan it out. You don't have to manipulate it into happening. Your job . . . let go. Your job . . . rest. Your job . . . trust."

"Your job . . . let go. Your job . . . rest. Your job . . . trust."

Some days being a dreamer is hard. But then I remember dreams bring me closer to my Father. Dreams make my heart dance. Dreams get me on my knees. Dreams cause me to seek after Jesus. Dreams remind me that God is good and fun and powerful. He's got everything covered. Sometimes we just need to be okay with the fact that we feel a little frustrated in the wait. It's all right. We're doing fine. Keep waiting. It takes big faith to wait.

What does waiting feel like to you? For me, waiting feels like my mind can't fully rest. It's like the feeling I would get in the ballet studio when I was trying to learn a new piece of choreography.

Until the choreography completely gelled in my mind, it was unsettling not knowing the steps. Being in that position is a place of limbo for a dancer. But, oh, how sweet the rehearsal day was when it all gelled! When the choreography finally stuck in my brain and then the muscle memory kicked in, I could fully enjoy dancing.

As we wait in real life, we can remember that God does not want us to live in a state of emotional stress and anxious limbo. This waiting is a dance of learning to trust God with everything in our lives. He wants us to live free of angst and worry as we wait for Him to unfold our dreams. Waiting is a reminder to trust in His timing, His ways, and His plan.

As I wait, I know I need to let go of my old habitual ways of processing (checking my email a zillion times, escaping into information overload hoping the answer will appear, getting stressed and antsy) and make room for the new, healthy perspective that waiting can be an ideal time to draw closer to Jesus.

God's got you. God's got me. God's got plans for your life. He knows every detail. He knows what is best. He's at work behind the scenes. I like to think He's most actively at work on your behalf particularly on the days you feel as though your prayer requests may have gone unnoticed. His love for you is deep, personal, and ever-pursuing. He's passionate about you, and He has surprises up His sleeve and just around the corner. The challenge is not to rush Him but to trust that His timing is best. It will be worth the wait. He will answer, and then your heart will dance with joy as you look back and see how He worked for your good. But in the meantime, He invites you to start dancing now and live as though He's going to bring the dreams He has planned for you to fruition.

He's the God of joy, and He wants you to live joyfully even during the waiting. The more you remind yourself that He has everything covered, the more your heart will gel with His peace.

When It Feels Like God Doesn't Hear You

As you wait on your dreams, there may be moments when you wonder if God hears your prayers. Sometimes it can feel like He doesn't hear you or like your prayers are silly. In the waiting, keep praying. Keep taking your thoughts to Him. Because as you continue to pray, even when it feels like the answer is far off, you draw closer to Him as you cry out. God is listening and He hears you. The answer is on the way. It may look different from the answer you were hoping for or it may be exactly the same, but either way, it's riding the waves of His perfect timing. He is never early. He is never late.

> God is listening and He hears you.

I also want to encourage you (literally, give you courage) not to despair (lose hope, give up) in the wait. Focus on Him. It's so easy to let doubt and anxiety creep in, making you trust God less and less. It's easy to forget how trustworthy God is and to start taking matters into your own hands, as if His timetable is not fast enough. I love God's message to us in the following verses:

> I don't think the way you think. The way you work isn't the way I work . . . For as the sky soars high above earth, so the way I work surpasses the way you work, and the way I think is beyond the way you think. (Isa. 55:8–9 Message)

Waiting for a dream to unfold or a prayer to be answered can feel like watching a garden grow. When we watch constantly for something to change, it can seem as if nothing is happening and progress is going to take forever. Sometimes a dream, like a garden, can appear to be an impossible pursuit or a completely hopeless desire. We want our dream to feel like a beautiful rose blooming in all its glory, but instead it feels like a bud—closed up and dormant. But remember that a bud has the potential to become something beautiful.

Let God speak to you in the wait. I encourage you to write a little note to yourself from God, imagining what He might say to you in your own dance of waiting. Write down the things you want to remember in your waiting moments. For example:

> I love you so much that you can let your dream go and hold it up to Me. Let Me take care of you, let Me work it out. When you start to get anxious, pray—talk to Me. Let go and let Me work. Be at peace because I know what is best for you, and it may or may not be what you are hoping for. It might be something far better!

I picture God smiling down on you—hardly able to contain His excitement for the plans, joys, and blessings He has for you. The wait will be worth it.

Holding on to Hope

As we encourage a garden to grow by providing it with water, we nurture a dream or request by showering it with prayer and nourishing it by surrendering it into God's hands over and over again. And then one day we come across our little garden of a dream and it's blooming and growing; all the flowers are mounding together to create a breathtaking scene—and our dream begins to flourish. The beauty was unfolding all the while we thought nothing was happening.

I know you can't see the end result of your dreams, but God can. He has plans and knows how He's going to work everything out. He's got you. He's got this.

Recently as I navigated some of my own waiting angst, I felt myself teetering between keeping my hopes up or simply giving up. *Would it be easier just to stop dreaming?* I wondered. Then a friend emailed me about similar questions going on in her heart. "I am afraid to hope, you know?" she wrote. Yes. I know. Sometimes when our hopes don't turn out the way we want, well, it hurts. So sometimes we stop hoping or dreaming because we don't want to feel that pain. But here's what I also know: keeping our hopes down keeps our joy down; it robs us of peace, energy, and excitement. I think of this verse: "Hope deferred makes the heart sick, but a longing fulfilled is a tree of life" (Prov. 13:12).

> Keep your hope planted firmly in the Master Gardener, who is diligently gardening your dreams and requests.

Hope deferred (put off, delayed) makes the heart sick, but a longing fulfilled (keeping that hope in God) is a tree of life (a thriving, well-established, growing, healthy soul). And so wherever you are in life, whatever dreams you are waiting on, whatever answer you are waiting for, rest assured that intricate happenings are going on behind the scenes that you can't see. A Master Gardener is working things out on your behalf. Even though it feels like nothing good is happening in the waiting, buds are getting ready to bloom. Subtle blossoms are emerging. Keep your hope planted firmly in the Master Gardener, who is diligently gardening your dreams and requests.

Prayer, Scripture, and Reflection
for Your Dreaming Heart

Lord, help me live joyfully in the wait. Let my heart keep dancing in trust and hope that You're working out the details behind the scenes in ways that are far better than my plans.

_____

_____

_____

_____

_____

_____

"The LORD is a refuge for the oppressed, a stronghold in times of trouble. Those who know your name trust in you, for you, LORD, have never forsaken those who seek you." Psalm 9:9–10

"Be still before the LORD and wait patiently for him." Psalm 37:7

"I wait for the LORD, my whole being waits, and in his word I put my hope." Psalm 130:5

_____

_____

_____

_____

1. What dreams are you waiting for?

_____

_____

_____

2. How do you typically handle the waiting seasons?

3. How has the waiting been hard?

4. What secures your hope in your own waiting season?

5. How might your waiting seasons deepen your intimacy with the Lord?

de-
1. Clutter & simply
2. Gods best for us?
3. How know?

7

° °

Simplifying Your Life Down to God's Best Assignments

Let us throw off everything that hinders and the sin that so easily entangles. And let us run with persever-ance the race marked out for us.

Hebrews 12:1

Wherever we are in our dreaming journeys, it's important to simplify our lives down to the roles and dreams He has specifically planned for us. When we don't, our dreaming journey quickly becomes a stressful and distracted one.

Looking to God to Clarify Your Roles

Simplifying is a beautiful thing. We all know the feeling of clar-ity that comes when we declutter our closets or purses or cars. We function better because we can find what we need easily and quickly. In our dreaming journeys, we often take on more roles, jobs, obligations, and activities than God intends for us to carry. As a result, we need to simplify our lives down to God's best plans and dreams for us. When we do, we thrive in the roles and dreams He has created for us.

A ballet dancer is constantly trying to cut out the bad habits in her dancing in order to dance her best. All the extras that naturally creep into a dancer's technique become distracting to the audience, taking away from the beauty and simplicity of clean ballet technique. When a dancer focuses on only the essentials of proper technique, her dancing reaches new heights. Just as extra wiggles and bobbles in a dancer's ballet technique take away from her dancing, when our lives become overloaded with extra responsibilities, distractions, comparing thoughts, or information overload, these things keep us from thriving in the roles and dreams God has for us.

Mr. Truman Finney, one of my ballet teachers, gave me a clear picture of the need for simplicity in my dancing—and, really, in my everyday life. Mr. Finney quickly became one of my favorite teachers because of his quiet nature, his smile that meant you were doing something right, and the way he respected the art of ballet. He would simplify the music down to just the chords of the piano and the snapping of his fingers.

Mr. Finney loved horses (be still, my heart!) and compared our technique and training to the beauty of a style of horseback riding called "dressage," which means "horse ballet." The horse holds its head beautifully and is completely attentive to the rider. The rider directs and guides the horse with a light nudge or by putting slight pressure on the horse's bridle to guide the horse in every detail, including which foot the horse should put forward. The horse's steps are organized and clean—there are no extra bobbles or steps. Mr. Finney wanted us to "cut away" or "cut out" all the extra stuff from our dancing. Habits such as checking the mirror, unnecessary fidgeting, and wiggling to get into position

Simplicity — Not perfection

needed to go. The placement of our feet and arms had to be exact, precise, and clear-cut. This focus on simplicity led to growth. I grew stronger, and I enjoyed the effort of simplifying. Although it may sound restrictive, focusing on the basics of my technique and cutting out all the extra distractions and bad habits was freeing. Staying in those boundaries of the technique I knew, just as a horse stays within the boundaries of its bridle, freed me up to get stronger and become a cleaner dancer. Mr. Finney passed away not too long ago, and I will always feel indebted to him for helping me grow as a dancer.

In life, often we default to answering yes after yes after yes, without really seeking God about our yeses. Our stress and fast pace keep us from thriving, making life frustrating and overwhelming. God wants to ease our load by helping us realize that less is more. He wants to do some maintenance within us to realign our hearts with His. He knows my capacity and my schedule—He knows it all. While I go running off like the wind trying to handle too much, juggle it all, and add even more things to my life, He's quietly waiting for me to seek Him in everything. He loves to help me live well. He loves to help me sort things out to keep me from spreading myself too thin. My default mode is to try to do too many things. He protects me from my own good intentions. Sometimes when something doesn't work out the way I want it to, I have to trust God has a simpler plan in mind and find the beauty in simplicity.

His Best Assignments

Part of dreaming with God is simplifying our lives down to His very best assignments for us.

We make room for God's very best assignments for us by looking to Him to define and clarify our roles. Just as a ballet dancer dances many roles throughout her dancing days, we as women live out various roles in our lives. We juggle this dance of being different things at different times to different people. Over the years, my roles in life have been ballet dancer, ballet teacher, wife, mom, writer, speaker, daughter, sister, friend, and volunteer. Add in cook, carpool driver, housekeeper, and errand runner and you get the idea—life gets busy and full. But sometimes when we spread ourselves too thin trying to fulfill different roles, we miss out on living out the roles God really wants us to hone in on. So how do we know what roles we should focus on? We bring all of them to God

> Part of dreaming with God is simplifying our lives down to His very best assignments for us.

and ask God for guidance. He nudges us toward His best for us.

I have felt God's simplifying nudges in my own dreaming journey many times. My three precious boys have my heart completely, and God has nudged my heart time after time to keep my life as simple as possible so that I can thrive in motherhood and have the energy to love them well. Learning to discern how many roles I can juggle with motherhood has been a process for sure. During some seasons, I attempted to dance, teach ballet, write, volunteer at the boys' school, and be Mom all at the same time. While it was fun, I often felt spread too thin. God would nudge my heart as if to say, "It's okay, Sarah. You don't have to do it all and be it all. It's okay to simplify."

> He nudges us toward His best for us.

Looking back, I see that God's nudges to simplify are always to the benefit of my own sense of peace and well-being, my family, and my relationship with Him. Simplifying down to God's best assignments helps us thrive in the roles and dreams God has for us.

Our roles will shift and change throughout our lives, and we navigate those shifts by bringing them to God. He steers with His nudges. He clarifies. Sometimes He nudges through the excitement we feel for a role, but often He nudges through the dread we feel for a role. There will be times when we feel obligated to do something or be someone that's not really in line with God's best for us. We can take that sense of dread we feel to the Lord, and oftentimes, we will see He is doing clarifying work.

Understanding Your Capacity

Part of simplifying our lives down to God's best is understanding our capacities. Some of us function well when our lives are busy and full of activity, and some of us get totally overwhelmed juggling too many things. We figure out where we land on the spectrum through trial and error, and God delights in helping us learn how we are wired.

Do you flourish in busyness or do you wilt? Are you inspired by a full calendar or do you get completely overwhelmed? Here's the thing: our capacities are different because we are all uniquely wired. God wants us to operate within our unique capacities. When we do this, we have the energy and time to live exactly as God has called us to.

One way to learn what our capacities are and how to live within them is by bringing our calendars to God, weighing our decisions carefully, and learning to say no. God wants in on our everyday lives because every day is part of the sweet dance of dreaming with Him. He wants us to weigh our decisions carefully through prayer so we have the energy, time, and space to pursue Him and the dreams and roles He has for us. He wants us to know we don't have to say yes to everything, and He helps us graciously say no when we need to.

> God wants us to operate within our unique capacities.

All this simplifying down to God's best means letting go of our do-it-all mentalities so we can operate in true peace, joy, and strength. Simplifying down to God's best is deciphering His roles, schedules, and pursuits for us. Sometimes the process includes letting go of a role and sometimes it involves stepping out into a new role. That's the dance of getting to God's best. It isn't always pretty, but the clarifying we experience is worth it.

When I prune my life down to doing only the things that I truly feel God has guided me to do, my heart dances its dance seemingly right in tune with God—as if I'm in that perfect spot of the sweetest dance He made for me and Him. My human tendency is to add on extra activities and commitments and projects and ideas, but when I rest in the fact that I don't need more to do than God's perfect dance for me, my soul dances, my life feels simpler, and my joy overflows. When we simplify our lives down to His best, we flourish in the dreams He has for us.

> With a clear focus on God, we dance our dreaming dances with a beautiful sense of purpose and the deep comfort of knowing who we are in Him.

As we come to this place of simplifying our lives down to God's best, we have more capacity to thrive in the roles and dreams He has for us. With a clear focus on God, we dance our dreaming dances with a beautiful sense of purpose and the deep comfort of knowing who we are in Him.

The secret to thriving in the roles and dreams God has for us is releasing comparison, tuning out distractions, staying inspired, and cultivating gratefulness.

Breaking Free from Comparison Mode

The ballet studio, the playground, the soccer field, the mall, the grocery store, the party, the baby shower . . . you name it, people are comparing themselves to others. It's natural for us to do this, but it can also do great damage to our lives. In fact, I believe it's one of the biggest obstacles to our living out joy-filled, abundant lives and following the dreams God has for us.

In these situations where we compare how we measure up to others, we're left feeling not good enough, not pretty enough, not wealthy enough, not "together" enough . . . the list goes on and on. Our comparing ways wreak havoc on our dreaming hearts.

I often felt the temptation to compare myself to the other dancers the minute I walked into the ballet studio. The floor-to-ceiling mirrors did not help ward off this temptation either. I secretly hoped that the mirrors would magically make me look better than I did the day before. Maybe today would be the day I would watch myself dance and think, *Wow! You're a beautiful dancer! Don't change a thing!* But no, my reflection only stared back at me self-consciously and sometimes even attempted to convince me to quit dancing. After I slipped on my ballet shoes and did some stretches and sit-ups to warm up, I would try to remember to get my focus right.

This helped for a moment or two. I would often start out feeling good about my dancing and my body, but the second I saw a dancer performing better or looking better, my self-confidence would slowly crouch lower and lower. I could walk into class feeling gung ho and confident but finish feeling defeated and on the verge of throwing my pointe shoes out the window. Why? Because I let it all get to me? Yes. But more important, I realize now that I was focused more on how I measured up to others instead of appreciating how God made me. By constantly comparing myself to other dancers, I was wandering way off track from my dreaming journey.

God wants to keep you on track so you can rest in His truths that you are one of a kind to Him and that His roles and dreams for your life are one of a kind. It may feel like others have the exact same dreams or plans that you do. In the world's eyes, it may appear as if your dreams are common, or you might question your purpose because it feels like you're a carbon copy of another woman. At times you may feel simply . . . like a normal gal—not an extraordinary one. But please remember *you are extraordinary to God*. You are incredibly unique to God.

When you fall into this comparison mode (which will come and go), when you question yourself because you see others who seem more fit, more talented, more qualified, more whatever it is, hold on to this truth: God assigns you to your calling because it's the perfect fit for you. Recognize when you're starting to compare yourself to others. Acknowledge when you're starting to emotionally slide downhill because you're losing your confidence. And know that if you do feel yourself slipping, God will be there to catch you and lift you up.

As God brings you back to the joy of keeping your focus on Him and the callings He has for you, He will help you celebrate others in their unique callings. During the challenging moments when you feel yourself wondering if you're special, if you have anything to offer to the world, if God will use you, let your heart be sensitive to others around you who might feel the same way. Be the one to encourage another woman in her dreams. Be the one to remind her that God will guide her too. That He has unique plans for her life. Encouraging others in their callings is a beautiful part of dreaming with God.

One summer my husband whisked me away with him to California on a work trip. While he was finishing up a meeting, I sat in a hotel lobby and dove into my current writing project, which included writing this chapter about comparison. A water feature stood in the middle of the room, holding tall statues of angelesque women grouped in pairs. They were all holding up huge bowls of water that trickled down into a large pool. No one statue was prettier than the others. They were all on even ground, holding up the water together. Watching that beautiful water feature, I realized that, like the statues, we, as daughters of Christ, are all needed to hold up the Living Water so it can flow out to the people who need it. It occurred to me what an honor it is to be used by the Source to offer up His water to thirsty souls. When we dream with God, He uses us in our own unique ways to bring His Living Water to those around us. He doesn't have to use us, but He wants to. He has such an abundance of holy water to get to thirsty souls that He needs many messengers. Our work as His messengers is ultimately what our call to dream with Him is all about. But when we get caught up in comparing ourselves to others, the flow of His Living Water slows.

Comparison depletes our hearts, leaving us with less enthusiasm, energy, efficiency, and excitement for our callings. It robs us of our kingdom purposes. Every day is a battle to keep our hearts glued to Jesus. We make a million little choices regarding where we will focus our energy. I long to focus on God and His mission and dreams for me instead of piddling away potentially great moments because I'm consumed with comparing myself to others. I don't want to be the funny woman statue whose bowl is tipped over and empty because she is too busy peering over at her gal statue friends, wishing she were them. I don't want to miss out on becoming all that God created me to be because I'm so focused on who someone else is becoming and how she compares to me. Comparison loses its grip on us when we see that we're actually working together as a whole for His kingdom. Sometimes just recognizing when we are in comparison mode, noting its damaging effect and pausing to let God center us back on Him, helps us fully break free from it.

> When we get caught up in comparing ourselves to others, the flow of His Living Water slows.

This idea of re-centering makes me think of ballet class. One of the most vital benefits of class is how it centers the dancer both physically and mentally. Sometimes when I entered the studio, my body felt sore, tight, weak, and tired. I would not have dreamed of throwing on my tutu and pointe shoes in that physical state because my body was not properly warmed up. In addition, mentally, I was not in an enthusiastic place because of my sore, aching muscles. Hopping into a full day of rehearsal with a bad attitude was never a good idea. To be prepared for the full load of rehearsals ahead for the day, I needed to center my thoughts back to a good place, remembering that I was doing what I loved despite the fact that my body hurt.

Upon stepping into the studio to begin my warm-up routine, I started to feel myself becoming more centered physically and mentally. Before class began, I would get cozy in my favorite warm-up attire, find a spot at the barre, and begin to warm up my body. I loved to put on my headphones and do some stretching and conditioning to wake up my muscles. Typically, I jammed to my praise and worship music because I could use all the help I could get to center my thoughts and my heart on God's truth in those moments when I was tired, sore, or slipping into comparison mode. As the music poured into my ears, the weight of negative thoughts began to lift, and I remembered God was with me. There was no need to compare dancing abilities or body shapes; instead I could just enjoy the gift of dancing.

After some abdominal and inner-thigh exercises, I usually moved on to an easy set of push-ups, which got my blood flowing and my heart rate up. Last, I did all kinds of stretches that prepared my muscles to work hard and helped prevent injuries. As I went through this process, my muscles became engaged and my mind began to drift into a peaceful zone of concentration. Also, my heart and attitude were in a good place again after focusing on God instead of the comparison trap. It was a wonderful feeling!

When class began and the teacher started to lead us through each combination of pliés, tendues, dégagés, and ronds de jambe (or rootie toos, as my husband likes to call them) at the barre, my body would begin to lengthen and strengthen. My muscles loosened up and became more flexible as I found my center of gravity. This was a process, but it was so incredible to feel centered, long, tall, and grounded all at the same time. After barre, we moved to the center of the studio. At this point we had to depend fully on our center of gravity by engaging our core abdominal muscles and lengthened bodies from all the preparation at the barre. After an entire class, we were centered, properly warmed up, and ready for rehearsals and performances.

Like ballet class centers a dancer for a rehearsal day or performance, Christ centers all of us for the big stage of everyday life. No matter the comparing thoughts racing through our minds, we can always turn to Him. Remember that spending time with Jesus is how we find the nurturing, encouragement, joy, and fulfillment we need to thrive in the roles and dreams He has just for us. When we feel depleted, we can seek Him. He will set our hearts, thoughts, and emotions right again, leaving us feeling refreshed, ready, and rejuvenated.

Just as dancers finish class feeling energized, strong, centered, and ready to perform, Christ energizes, strengthens, and centers us. The remedy for switching out of comparison mode is staying centered on Christ. He keeps us there. He reins us in when we drift. He signals a little alarm in our hearts when we are wandering off. We will always be tempted to take our eyes and hearts off the Lord, but with His help, we can remain fixated on Him. He loves us so personally that He tugs on our hearts to keep them tightly woven to His. As He centers us and helps us break free from comparison mode, we grow strong and grounded in our roles.

> As He centers us and helps us break free from comparison mode, we grow strong and grounded in our roles.

Tuning Out Distractions and Tuning In to God

Another way that we thrive in our roles is by tuning out distractions and guarding our hearts. We must filter what comes into our minds and hearts on a daily, moment-by-moment basis. What's coming into your mind and heart each day? Here are some examples from my own life:

> *Lists.* To-do lists, grocery lists, reminders, dates, and on and on (lots of sticky notes going on in my house).
>
> *Information overload.* Emails, newsfeeds from Facebook and Instagram, news on the TV, or a good read from another blogger.
>
> *Requests and pressure to make quick decisions.* Opportunities to volunteer and invitations to birthday parties, showers, and school events, which produce feelings of guilt if I have to say no to these requests. (Ugh!)
>
> *Mindless distraction.* Checking my phone for interesting stuff, including texts (which I love because they are usually from family members and friends) and emails (again).
>
> *Unbridled thoughts and worries.* Not mature enough, not pretty enough, not a good enough mom, not a good enough wife, not skinny enough, not this, not that . . . you know the drill. Worrying about this thing and that thing and this person and that situation. My thought patterns can wear me out.
>
> *Discontentment.* Looking around and suddenly having a strong desire for that new purse/leotard/dress/haircut because I feel not enough.

What do all these lists, requests, information, and thoughts do to our hearts? Personally, I feel myself sinking ever so slightly emotionally into a web of distraction. This sinking is subtle and slowly robs me of joy and peace. Each new, unfiltered thought or piece of information that piles onto my already heavy load pushes me deeper into stress, anxiety, and an overall feeling of inner turmoil. These distractions squander my contentment, causing me to feel fragmented and lost. I feel numb to life. I lose my footing and start to question and even forget my purpose and the value of my roles as a mom, wife, dancer, or writer. It doesn't feel good. My thoughts vanish in a vast cloud of information, putting me into a funk. When I'm distracted, it's as though I'm too distracted to keep dancing forward. Life feels like a list rather than a dance.

I love my cell phone, but I often feel it's a distraction from my walk with God and dancing in the direction of the dreams God is leading me in. When I find myself a bit too preoccupied with my little device, I know it by the way my heart starts to feel more and more on empty. It's funny, because I will see technology take over too much in the lives of my kiddos before I see it in my own life. They don't have phones yet, but they have devices to play games on and television, of course. This past summer, our family headed to Missouri for family camp. On our annual date night at a local Mexican restaurant (yes, this gal has a heart for guacamole and chips), the topic of our kids' technology use seemed to burst from my heart and land right in Brian's lap.

I was so tired of battling with my boys about how much screen time was enough—or too much. I knew the answer was not to ban technology completely, although, if Brian had suggested that, I would have been on board, I think. As Brian and I started to discuss the issue, we realized we hadn't laid down any firm boundaries for the boys. They didn't know when they were allowed to play a game on a device or to watch a show. So we came up with some rules about when they were allowed to use their devices.

We were both kind of hesitant to announce these new rules to our boys because we were afraid they would see us as "mean Mommy and Daddy." But when we came home from dinner, we took a couple deep breaths and laid out the new boundaries—and guess what? The boys got excited, dare I even say giddy! Having boundaries freed them up to enjoy their technology without being tied to it and without getting in trouble when they used it. We were a little skeptical of their excitement, but we put our little plan into place and I'm so happy to report that they are thriving in it. They know their boundaries, as do Brian and I, and it's no longer a tiresome battle. Of course, it's not perfect either, but it's much better. I know technology use will be an ongoing discussion as they grow older, but this situation taught me about the goodness of boundaries and an unplugged life.

As I've watched my boys thrive amid these new technology boundaries, I've had many aha moments regarding my own technology use. Plain and simple, I feel closer to God, my husband, and my boys when I'm fully present. Also, I feel more in my own dreaming journey when I'm not scrolling through a newsfeed. In other words, an unplugged life helps me thrive in the roles and dreams God has given me.

So God and I do this dance of laying down some boundaries for my own heart. I find that the more I stay in the boundaries that work for me, the more peaceful I feel and the less I have to battle distraction. And it feels so good! So much good information is available at our fingertips, but I know I have to be careful not to overwhelm my mind with too much because I become disconnected from my life, God's good purposes for me, and even God Himself.

Unplugging truly slows us down and helps us get right back in tune with God and embrace who we are and where God has us. Answering the call on our lives to dream with God requires that we be incredibly in tune with Him. A great step toward tuning in to God is tuning out all our distractions and devices and immersing ourselves in Scripture, making room for quiet moments of prayer and stillness before the Lord.

God's Word and presence fill us like nothing else can. He satisfies any hunger inside us for purpose, comfort, and encouragement.

His Word guides our hearts and thoughts and reminds us that we are His daughters. God clears the fog of information overload as we turn away from our distractions and toward Him. He de-stresses our souls as we look solely to Him. When we drink in His Word and linger with Him in moments of prayer and stillness, our hearts grow more in tune with Him and to His dreams for us.

Below are a few simple and practical ideas for tuning out distractions.

> Answering the call on our lives to dream with God requires that we be incredibly in tune with Him.

Rewire our habits. We set ourselves up for distraction when we have a momentary lull in life. Maybe it's waiting in the carpool line or at the doctor's office or being stuck in traffic. The only thing interesting in our purses is our phones, so we pull them out and scroll, scroll, scroll, check, check, check. Lots of information weaves through our minds all at once, feeding our stress. Our in-between moments end up depleting us instead of filling us. But instead we can choose to rewire our habits so that those lulls in life become life-giving. We can try keeping a Bible, Scripture verses on index cards, or a devotional book in our purses. Then we can reach for those instead of our phones during those in-between moments. Or we can use those moments to linger with God in prayer and stillness. We can check in with Him instead of checking our phones. (I know that's much easier said than done!)

Set boundaries. We can avoid distraction by setting boundaries for when we check the news and our email and social media. Figure out what time of day works best for you, commit to a time frame, and then be done with it. Also, keep your phone and computer in a place where you're not constantly walking past them so you will not be tempted to check them outside your set time frame. If you notice that following certain people or accounts on social media causes you to feel less-than or stirs up discontentment, guard your heart by choosing to unfollow them. Otherwise, comparison rears its icky head easily, as we talked about before, and keeps you from flourishing in your roles.

Declare a fast. There is something freeing about taking a total break from social media or email or whatever it is that's distracting you from your life. Taking a break, whether it's for a few hours, a day, a weekend, a week, or a couple of months, gives your soul and heart space to feast on the presence of God, soak in His Word more deeply, and enjoy His company more fully. In addition, we grow more in tune to the gift of our lives and the gifts of the people around us. When we recognize that our souls are growing more and more depleted from our distractions, we would be wise to give them a rest by declaring a fast. When we unplug, our hearts plug back into God, and hearts plugged into God are hearts enjoying abundant life.

When we tune out distractions and put God's presence and Word first in our lives, we thrive, staying on course with His dreams for us.

I often sit between this tension of wanting to live out God's dreams for me with great gusto and confidence and feeling discouraged because I'm distracted. So instead of moving forward in my dreams and living my daily life with intention, I sit stuck in between. God always seems to share His truths with me when I get to this tense place and reminds me to let go of my distracted ways. He wakes me up and helps me take on my dreams and my daily life with new inspiration as I curl in close to Him through His Word. He wants to do the same for all of us. He is our Helper and Counselor in all things, even in this battle to overcome the distractions of this world.

Staying Inspired

Staying inspired is another important key to us thriving in our roles and the dreams God has for us. Sometimes our dreaming hearts just plain forget about the beauty of our unique dreams. On the days we lose a bit of our zeal, we need a little reminder to keep us stepping toward our dreams. Staying inspired keeps our hearts on course.

When I was dancing, one of the somewhat silly ways I stayed inspired was to ask my mom and dad for new leotards for my birthday. (Dancers, you get this!) I should mention I did this well into my thirties. New leotards made me giddy and excited to get back into the studio. Wearing something different than my usual go-to rehearsal wardrobe brought a freshness and newness to my dancing dream. (Thank you, Mom and Dad.)

> When we tune out distractions and put God's presence and Word first in our lives, we thrive, staying on course with His dreams for us.

Another way I stayed inspired during my dancing years was to watch the performance videos that my dad and Brian had recorded. Something about seeing the whole process come together into the performance kept my heart inspired and motivated on the much less glamorous rehearsal days. It reminded me that the opportunity to dance professionally was special and that even when it felt too hard some days, the performances always made the struggle worth it.

> Staying inspired keeps our hearts on course.

Our dreams could easily become a grind. As many of us know, our real-life responsibilities, such as cooking meals, doing the dishes, cleaning the house, driving the kids to their activities, responding to school emails, and so forth can kind of wear down our hearts and cause us to forget their value and importance. One way I stay inspired as a wife and mom is simply by reminding myself of the value of these roles. Sometimes I need to pause and consider what a beautiful and high calling these gigs are. I need to remember that these are my greatest dreams come true. In caring for and loving these guys, I'm participating in holy and good work. My investment in them is the sweetest part of dreaming with God. A perspective check and a little heart pep talk keep me inspired in marriage and motherhood. In practical terms, quality time with Brian, whether it's a date night out or drinking coffee together on our back porch, reminds me that this togetherness in marriage is my greatest dream come true. Also, as I mentioned before, our little family heads to Missouri every summer for family camp. Taking a short hiatus from chores, busy calendars, and everyday routines seems to freshly inspire me. During this time away, the love of my heavenly Father whispers to me and washes such beautiful grace and truth over me, reminding me that my marriage and family is of utmost value. There I find precious inspiration to keep dreaming with God.

As a writer, I stay inspired through various ways. One of my favorite sources of inspiration is the bookstore. With a coffee cup in hand, inspiration and excitement for writing swells up inside me as I browse the aisles and aisles of books. Sometimes if I'm feeling discouraged, a trip to the bookstore perks me up and reminds me that writing is one of God's unique dreams for me and that even though the process can feel slow or self-doubt can try to steal my joy, God is with me through it all.

Reading is another way I stay inspired as a writer. I buy way too many books and read multiple books at once. Keeping a good read close by reminds me that the whole writing and publishing process eventually becomes the gift of a book in someone else's hand just as the rehearsal process in dancing eventually becomes a performance. This thought makes me incredibly giddy.

Also, I stay inspired to keep dreaming with God and appreciate the roles He has given me by keeping motivating reminders nearby. For instance, when I was dancing, laying out my stage makeup on a floral print towel, all nice and orderly, and placing pictures of my family on the mirror in front of me kept me inspired as I sat backstage preparing for a show. In marriage and motherhood, my home is a source of inspiration for me: pictures hang on the walls, purple homemade cards from my boys decorate my desk, cards from my husband cover my nightstand, and old journals line the bookshelf in our bedroom. To stay inspired in my writing, I pin encouraging quotes to my bulletin board, keep a stack of favorite books next to me as I work, and of course, make sure to have a good cup of coffee nearby. All these physical reminders of God's faithfulness in leading me to my unique roles keep me inspired and help me truly enjoy these roles.

So I encourage you to find your own unique ways to stay inspired in your own dreaming journey.

Cultivating Gratefulness

Staying inspired helps us cultivate gratefulness for who God made us to be and the dreams He planted in us. He longs for us to love where He has us. Gratefulness gets us to that place. Gratefulness also points our hearts to the One who is the ultimate Dreamer— God Himself. Gratefulness reminds us that this dreaming dance is all about Him. As we cultivate gratefulness, thriving in our roles becomes much, much easier. As we soak in all that God has done for us in our own dreaming dances, we start to "own" our dances, so to speak. When we own our dances, God's best assignments including the roles and dreams He has just for us, we flourish.

Whether your dreaming journey involves big stages with lights and audiences or the quietness of home where no one notices the details you take care of, remember that your callings matter. Your work, your dreaming with God, what you do is spiritual work. Your callings are your mission field.

You delight God and make Him smile by embracing your roles and His dreams for you and doing what He created you to do. I encourage you to break free from the comparison mode and your tendencies to get lost in the world's distractions and instead get to know God in a deeper way. Stay inspired in the things He has called you to in this life and find ways to keep your feet grounded in gratefulness. Your roles are absolutely significant, and God wouldn't want you doing anything else but dancing through life in the dreams He has for you.

> Your callings are your mission field.

Prayer, Scripture, and Reflection
for Your Dreaming Heart

Take my heart and simplify it so that I have more room to know You and to do only the things You're calling me to do. Show me what in my schedule and on my calendar needs to go and what needs to stay. Let me simplify my life so I can keep You as my main focus. May that focus be the source from which everything in my life flows. Thank You for bringing to light the comparison and distraction that goes on in my heart on a daily basis. Thank You for showing me how destructive these are to my heart, soul, and mind. Thank You for loving me so much and for directing me in the path to Your best for me. Lord, I lay down all the ways I compare myself in life and all the distractions

*that are keeping me from focusing on You. I ask for Your
divine help and grace to lay aside these distractions and
recognize the debilitating thoughts I think throughout the
day. In your strength and with Your guidance, help me live
differently. May my soul cling to You and enjoy the quiet,
deep rest that results from centering my life on You.*

_____

_____

_____

_____

_____

_____

"But my eyes are fixed on you, Sovereign LORD; in you I
take refuge." Psalm 141:8

"Above all else, guard your heart, for everything you do
flows from it." Proverbs 4:23

"You will keep in perfect peace those whose minds are
steadfast, because they trust in you." Isaiah 26:3

"The thief comes only to steal and kill and destroy; I have
come that they may have life, and have it to the full." John
10:10

"Do not conform to the pattern of this world, but be
transformed by the renewing of your mind. Then you will
be able to test and approve what God's will is—his good,
pleasing and perfect will." Romans 12:2

"Finally, brothers and sisters, whatever is true, whatever is noble, whatever is right, whatever is pure, whatever is lovely, whatever is admirable—if anything is excellent or praiseworthy—think about such things." Philippians 4:8

"Let us throw off everything that hinders and the sin that so easily entangles. And let us run with perseverance the race marked out for us." Hebrews 12:1

_____

_____

_____

_____

1. What roles do you sense God nudging you to simplify your life down to? What dreams and activities do you sense are His very best for you?

_____

_____

_____

2. What things have you said yes to that make you feel pressured, panicked, stressed, or just overwhelmed?

_____

_____

_____

3. What things can you say no to in order to free up your schedule to make room for more of God and His dreams for you?

_____

_____

_____

4. Note how it makes you feel when you're in "comparison mode."

_____

_____

_____

5. What personal distractions keep you from thriving in the roles and dreams God has for you?

_____

_____

_____

6. What are some practical ways you can eliminate comparison and distraction in your life?

_____

_____

_____

7. How can you stay inspired and cultivate gratefulness?

_____

_____

_____

8

○ ○

Seeing the Impact
of Dreaming with God

Let your light shine before others.

Matthew 5:16

We all long to know that our lives are full of purpose. We want assurance that each day matters. We want to feel purposeful in our passions and pursuits, in the grand things and the little details of our days that no one sees. Know this, dear reader: your spiritual journey of pressing into Christ will become the Holy Spirit's vehicle to impact and influence others. Your dreaming with God and thriving in the roles He has for you will bless others. Your purposes, roles, and callings were made for impact. As you dream with God, beauty will spill out in your everyday moments. You pursuing your dreams with God leading the way influences others for the kingdom.

Kingdom Moments Spilling Out

I remember one particular morning at a park when I ran into a friend and fellow young mom. We chatted and caught up with each other as we watched our little ones explore the jungle gym, swinging and climbing. She made me feel so loved by the way she asked very specific questions about how things were going in my life. She listened intently. Her gentle eyes made me feel important to her. I felt God's love for me through her. She didn't preach to me. She didn't pull out her Bible. She simply let God love through her. Her impact, I'm sure, was the result of her own dreaming journey with the Lord overflowing out onto me that day. She probably doesn't know how much that conversation meant to me, but she inspired me to see that when we dream with God and seek Him first, kingdom moments spill out into our everyday lives.

> When we dream with God and seek Him first, kingdom moments spill out into our everyday lives.

As we draw close to Christ in our dreaming journeys, He uses us to draw others to Him. It's a beautiful mystery how this works. We don't have to worry about how to make an impact on others because it will happen naturally as we pursue God; and it will happen in not only our dream-come-true moments but also our everyday moments. As we draw close to Him, beauty bursts through to others in a million little ways. The natural overflow of dreaming with God spills out in everyday moments like being an encouragement to our husbands, making breakfast for our kiddos with joy, hugging a friend who's down, writing a note to someone who needs support, or inspiring a fellow dreamer in their own dreams. Impacting others becomes a lifestyle as we press into Jesus. We may not even know we are having an effect on someone, just like that morning in the park. Your impact is a result of your heart seeking God.

I remember a time in my life when I wanted to clearly know my purposes and where God wanted me to make a difference for Him. I was gently reminded that in the pursuit of finding my specific purposes, my one and only purpose needed to be getting to know God. God slowly, over time, clarified His purposes for me, but He reminded me that His Spirit is the One who makes the impact through everyday moments.

When we make knowing God our primary focus, a beautiful thing happens—every moment becomes purposeful. Every task, every chore, every conversation, and every appointment becomes divine. When we see our moments as gloriously orchestrated by God, we live purposeful lives. We see God is involved in the little stuff and the big stuff. Each day holds different assignments. But everything has purpose. We don't have to worry whether we're making a difference; we can trust that the Spirit is at work through us and in us.

The Spirit at Work

I was with my family at a Christmas concert a while back. Twinkling lights lit up the stage, a full orchestra beautifully led the music, a grand piano sat front and center, and the singers brought all of us right into the Christmas spirit with their carols and songs.

One singer in particular who stood up to the microphone appeared quiet, almost shy, and maybe even a little bit nervous. She started singing softly and gently, and the whole crowd soon realized her voice was angelic. As the song unfolded, her voice reached a different realm. She had the most powerful and beautiful voice I had ever heard. Goose bumps covered my skin from head to toe, and something deep in my heart stirred. I remember thinking this woman clearly had a God-given, Spirit-filled gift. She didn't have to sell us on her voice. She didn't need someone to introduce her and set the stage for her. We didn't have to read her biography in the program. Her gift just came busting out. She was fully herself, and God's gifts came flowing from her to touch the audience. It made me think that that's how the Holy Spirit works when we walk in God's dreams for us. When we let Him guide our hearts and our lives, His Spirit comes busting out in ways that maybe we don't even realize.

This singer with the angelic voice will never know the effect she had on me, although I tried to let her know as I joined in with the thousands of audience members in a standing ovation. She will never know that somehow, in a way that I cannot put into words, the Holy Spirit reached right to my heart through her voice and blessed me. That's the Spirit's way—mysterious, angelic, powerful, moving. We can lean back, trusting that the Spirit is within us, working in mysterious ways and touching others in ways we don't realize, and that sometimes the most impactful moments are ones we may not even see. That divine movement of another's emotions, that stirring of someone else's heart—that's the Spirit at work.

> o o o o o
> That divine
> movement
> of another's
> emotions, that
> stirring of someone
> else's heart—that's
> the Spirit at work.
> o o o o o

It's easy to think that if we're not in ministry, then our "work" isn't as spiritual as it could be. I've gotten caught up in that line of thinking before, questioning my life as a professional ballerina. But, oh, how I had it all wrong. The Spirit can use each of us right where we are. We can be missionaries, soul-movers, and heart-stirrers wherever God has us. In dance, I couldn't use words on the stage, but my hope was that the Spirit would flow right out of my soul, through my piqué turns, and directly into the heart of even just one audience member.

When I was just eighteen years old and beginning my career with my first ballet company, I joined a small group Bible study through my church. The leader was a young mom, pregnant with her second baby, and we met one night a week at her home in the hills just on the outskirts of town. Those meetings became one of the highlights of my week. Driving through the hills to get to her house felt like a little getaway from the stress of the ballet world.

The minute I walked into her inviting home, she greeted me with a big hug, enthusiasm, and laughter and ushered me into her kitchen where the smell of chocolate brownies filled the air. Her red teakettle was always on the stove, singing its tune, announcing that hot chamomile tea was ours for the taking. The other gals and I kicked off our shoes and made ourselves comfy on her broken-in leather couches. Teacups in hand, we listened to our leader share her latest funny and endearing stories about life as a mom. We sipped on tea, snacked on brownies, and dove into God's Word together every week.

Somehow being in that house gave me a sense of comfort. Maybe because I was living in an apartment at the time, the walls of the house reminded me of the coziness of my childhood home. Somehow sipping that tea calmed me (and the teaspoonfuls of sugar did something sweet to my heart). Somehow my leader's joy and enthusiasm and cheerfulness for life, for us, and for God touched my soul. She set an example for me. She made me feel so welcome, and so loved. I felt God's love through her. Those weekly meetings became a sanctuary for me, a home away from home, an escape from the sometimes pressure-filled ballet world, and a place to get to know God better.

Looking back, I realize the Spirit was moving through my leader and loving on me in the meantime. The Spirit used the simplest things—a homey house, the smell of brownies, a hot cup of tea, sweet fellowship with other believers, and my leader—to bring me closer to Him. My leader didn't have to manufacture anything. It was all just the result of her own pursuit of God and dreaming with Him about how she could use her gifts to love others for Him. By pressing into Christ, the overflow of His love came streaming down on me. That's the beautiful mystery of the Spirit. I'm sure my Bible study leader loved to bake, loved to make her home a sanctuary, loved to teach God's Word, and loved being a mom. The Spirit gathered all those sweet delights of her heart, strung them together, and used the result to bless me and other young women who were hungry for God. It's so sweet. It's so good. The Spirit has a way . . . a way of stringing together the delights of our hearts for something we may not even realize is actually making an impact for God.

These memories make me think of my role as Mommy to my boys. I read them Bible verses and stories, play songs about Jesus for them in my car, and show them Bible-related DVDs, doing my best to answer their questions about faith, God, heaven, and walking with Jesus (they have lots of questions!). I try to do the right "spiritual" things to pass on my faith and incorporate it into our lives because there is something about the power of God's Word . . . hearing it, reading it. But some days not one Bible verse is spoken or read. Some days we learn more about superheroes than God. But I'm discovering (oh, and my heart constantly needs this reminder) that as I make knowing God my number one purpose, my boys will be impacted for Him. It may not look how I think it should some days, but that's okay. In fact, the Spirit can use many things to influence them for God. For instance, my oldest son may feel God's love through me as I listen to him rattle off facts and stats about the NFL. My middle son may feel God's love through me when I cook him a good meal and listen as he practices the guitar. My littlest guy loves when I simply swing with him out in our backyard. The Spirit's gentle,

> The Spirit has a way . . . a way of stringing together the delights of our hearts for something we may not even realize is actually making an impact for God.

divine touch is in and through it all. As we dream with God, the Spirit spills out of us, overflowing and touching others in ways we may not be able to put into words.

You Were Not Meant to Blend In

As a child of God and a dreamer with God, *you* are meant to be a light in the world. If you are walking with God, pursuing Him as He is pursuing you, studying His Word, and dreaming with Him, then you are going to stand out as a light. Not in a "famous" way . . . no, that's not what I mean . . . but in a God-size way.

Early in my dancing career, I worked hard to blend in with the other dancers. As part of the corps de ballet, my job was to look like, dance like, and move in perfect unison with the other dancers. I often received corrections to tone down my dancing so I would blend in better. I worked hard to dance smaller and make sure I didn't draw too much attention to myself. But then a funny thing started happening; every teacher, ballet master, and director started pushing me to "dance bigger." One particular ballet master quietly whispered to me with a grin across his face, "You were not meant to blend in." In that moment, he unofficially gave me permission to stop blending in and start dancing big. I felt giddy at the thought of dancing with a bit more abandon and freedom. Over the course of my dancing career though, my tendency was always to try to blend in, which sometimes felt easier and safer.

In life, we often try too hard to be like everyone else and do what everyone else is doing. Our tendency is to try to blend in, to go with the flow of everyone around us. Oftentimes in the studio, on the stage, or wherever I am in my daily life, I have to give myself a mental fist bump and remind myself, *You were not meant to blend in.* You are a follower of Jesus, pursuer of Christ, and dreamer with God, and as His Word gets in you and you get your heart in His Word, your life is going to look different. Your heart is going to look different; you will stand out not in a self-promoting way but in a drawing-people-to-Jesus way. And this is work that only the Spirit of God can do. I think of people in my life who stand out not because they are famous or boast of huge success or even have it all together but because they have a presence about them. A sweetness, a kindness, a gentleness, and a beauty.

These things are the fruit of the Holy Spirit in their lives. These people stand out, and they can't seem to help it. They are people such as my friend at the park and my Bible study leader, who stand out because of their joy and love and the way they give me a glimpse of Jesus. Oh, how I want to be a fruit-bearer. But I realize this doesn't just happen all on its own. Bearing fruit takes time, seasons of growth, pruning, and tending; it also takes spending time with God, trusting Him, praying to Him, obeying Him even when we would rather blend in, walking with Him, and letting the Spirit work inside us. When we dream with God, we bear fruit and God uses us to be a light in the world.

You are a light in the world. Press into Christ, because the result of seeking God and dreaming with Him is that you're going to look different. His light will radiate from inside you and shine for others to see. You were not meant to blend in; you were meant to shine for Him!

I pray you see today that God will use your dreaming with Him to impact others for His kingdom.

> You were not meant to blend in; you were meant to shine for Him!

Prayer, Scripture, and Reflection
for Your Dreaming Heart

Lord, thank You that You will use my pursuit of You to make a difference in others. I pray that as I seek You on a deeper level and begin to dream with You, Your Spirit will impact others through my life. I pray my life ultimately draws others into the intimacy and joy of knowing You. Thank You that Your Spirit is at work in me as I draw close to You.

_____

_____

_____

_____

_____

_____

"Let your light shine before others." Matthew 5:16

"But you will receive power when the Holy Spirit comes on you." Acts 1:8

"But thanks be to God, who always leads us as captives in Christ's triumphal procession and uses us to spread the aroma of the knowledge of him everywhere. For we are to God the pleasing aroma of Christ among those who are being saved and those who are perishing." 2 Corinthians 2:14–15

"You will shine among them like stars in the sky as you hold firmly to the word of life." Philippians 2:15–16

_____

_____

_____

_____

1. Can you think of a time when someone showed you the love of Christ in an everyday moment?

_____

_____

_____

2. In what ways that you have never thought of before might the Spirit be impacting others through your life?

_____

_____

_____

3. In what ways do you find yourself trying to blend in? How can you embrace letting your light shine?

_____

_____

_____

4. How does seeing the result of dreaming with God affect your perspective of the dreams He has for you?

_____

_____

_____

9

○ ○

Stirring Up Your Joy
for Your Daily Dance

Let them praise his name with dancing.

Psalm 149:3

It's our human nature to settle into a grind while we look forward to whatever our dreams may be. It's easy to slip into our daily routines, caught up in our to-do lists and responsibilities, all the while forgetting the joy of every day. We don't have to wait until the fulfillment of our dreams to be happy. How sweet is our God! He wants us to enjoy Him and our lives every single day. If our joy was dependent on our dreams being fulfilled, how unsteady our joy would be. Riding the waves of the journey to our dreams could potentially rock our emotions, deplete our joy, and send us into a grind. So in this chapter, we're going to stir up that joy in the journey. We're going to unpack what it looks like to savor our daily dances, our everyday dances, and in turn discover deep joy—no matter where we are on our dreaming journeys.

In a way, this reminds me of marriage. Before the wedding, we're all about bridal magazines, prepping for the big day, and planning the honeymoon. We can hardly wait until the day we get to begin a new life with our hubby. But if we aren't intentional about continuing to enjoy the everyday with our spouse, we can lose the joy of marriage! I know for Brian and me, some days the responsibilities, to-do lists, and cares of the day can outweigh the joy of "us." So we make sure we have fun too. And that's what I want to pinpoint in this chapter for you: I know I can get so serious about God sometimes that I forget He created laughter, fun, and joy. These were all His idea, so I'm convinced that part of the abundant life He has to offer us is a life of abundant joy. And this life is found not only on the days our dreams are fulfilled but also in the journey and the everyday.

What Makes You Giddy

Maybe you've lost your joy. Maybe you're not sure where it went. Or maybe you just feel like you have to battle more for it. I get that. The world doesn't make it easy to live with joy, and we do have an enemy who would love to steal it away from us. One check of the news can be such a downer. Darkness seems to be winning sometimes, doesn't it? I feel that weight too. Also, I know some of you have been through things I don't understand, things that are harder and deeper than I can speak to. Just know that, while I don't have words for the ache you feel, I love that you are here. All I can do is keep pointing you to the Lord because I do know this: He has the words, He has the comfort, and He has the love you need. While I don't know the depth of your pain, I know He is strong enough to help you through it. Thank you for being here.

I have found that one of the ways you can enjoy your journey is by tapping into what makes you giddy. By giddy, I mean light-hearted, joyful, and silly with excitement. What does that to you? What makes you forget about your email or your to-do list? The things that fill your heart to the brim and cause it to beat faster are the very things God uses to stir up your joy. But here's the thing: as we become more grown-up or start feeling like life has stolen our joy, sometimes we push those delights out of our lives, maybe without even meaning to. We settle into a rhythm of routines, responsibilities, and to-dos, and we forget to make time for the delights of our hearts. Now these are different from the dreams of our hearts. Delights are everyday things that feed our souls so we can savor and enjoy our daily dances no matter where we are on our dreaming journeys. Let me give you an example from my own life.

My dream to write is a big dream, and it has been quite a long journey filled with hurdles, delays, and detours along the way. This dream definitely makes me giddy, but I cannot depend on the fulfillment of this dream to keep my heart dancing every day. I cannot live for the day my first book is on the shelf, although you might find me dancing in the aisles of the bookstore on that day! I cannot stop the flow of joy and hold it all in until that day. I need giddiness today. It affects my marriage, my relationship with my kids, my mood, my attitude, my everything, and it refreshes me for my everyday dance. When I start pushing out the things that bring me joy and trade them in for simply plowing through my day, I lose my giddiness. And without it, I stop dreaming. Without it, I stop loving fully. Without it, I stop appreciating everyday moments.

My relationship with Jesus makes me giddy. I can't talk about giddiness without talking about Him. He overwhelms me with how good He is and how He not only saved us eternally but also lives in relationship with us. Jesus is the sweetest part of our dreaming journey and all our everyday moments. But, let me note, I can easily make my relationship with Him a chore or an obligation or another line on my to-do list if I'm not careful. So keeping my relationship with Jesus fresh is what brings me joy. We all have our own thing going on with the Lord, you know? Some of us like to meet with Him first thing in the morning, while some of us meet with Him right before bed. Some of us like reading plans, while some of us find them overwhelming. Some of us pray on walks, while some of us pray in stillness. My point is, each one of our relationships with Him is going to look different—and that's beautiful.

> Jesus is the sweetest part of our dreaming journey and all our everyday moments.

In a practical sense, here are some other things that make me completely giddy: speaking to groups of women and bringing them encouragement in their walk with the Lord, journaling, taking a long walk, gardening, reading a good book, hanging out with my three boys, and going on dates with my hubby. That's kind of the short list, but you get the idea. I need these things to keep my heart beating fast and to feel alive. What about you? What makes you giddy?

We touched earlier on how these desires can point to what we are made to do, but here we are focusing on how they can bring us joy in the day to day. Sometimes when I find myself in a little bit of a funk, perhaps stuck in the grind, I will notice that I haven't been doing many of these things. The minute I remember not just what makes me giddy but why these things are so important, a newness takes over in me. These things refresh, renew, and reenergize us. We become better versions of ourselves when we laugh, play, and have fun. When we tap into those things that are "us," we flourish. And God wants us to flourish. He wants us to enjoy life.

I realize you can't cast your routines, responsibilities, and work into the wind and go frolic through the wildflowers all day to keep your joy flowing, but is there a small step you could take today to tap into something that brings you joy? Could you take a long walk? Arrange some flowers? Take some photos? Build something? Design something? Get a massage? Play a game of tennis? Spend some time in your garden? Ski down a mountain? (I'm borrowing examples from my family of things that make them giddy. Love y'all . . . and I love how each of you are so uniquely wired.) What feeds your soul and how can you do a little more soul-feeding each day? When our souls are fed, our hearts come up from out of the grind. When we tap into our points of giddiness, we are savoring everyday life and stirring up our joy.

> When our souls are fed, our hearts come up from out of the grind.

Feeling God's Pleasure

When we do the things we love, we feel the pleasure of God in us and over us. Tapping into the way He wired us brings Him joy and we feel joy in return.

I can't really explain why I loved dancing professionally. All I know is that when I danced, I felt in tune with God's heartbeat for me. My limbs seemed to know what to do, and my heart seemed to function best when I danced. It's the same with motherhood. My heart loves it. I feel like I'm doing what I was made to do. And now with writing, it's not something I feel obligated to do. It's not something I have to sit down and make myself do; the words just swell up inside me and need a keyboard. I'm not saying writing is easy or doesn't have its hard moments, but it's something my heart feels wired to do—and so this heart and I, we write.

I think about family members again here: each of them taps into the things that either they love to do or that make them swell with creativity and I see the joy this brings them. This is true for Brian too. I love watching him build things. When he's out on the patio building something, he's not stressed out, he's filled up. He works with wood and tools not because he feels like he has to but because he wants to. I love that so much. When we do the things that bring us joy, we get a taste of God's pleasure.

Of course I have to mention the classic movie *Chariots of Fire*.

○ ○ ○ ○ ○

Make time for the things that allow you to feel God's pleasure.

○ ○ ○ ○ ○

"When I run, I feel God's pleasure." This line gets me every time I think about it because running doesn't seem like a spiritual thing, does it? But for Eric Liddell, running was spiritual. It put him in touch with God. Could it be that we feel God most when we do the things we were made to do? Could it be that we feel God's pleasure when we focus on the things we feel compelled to do, not obligated to do? Only God could be that creative. *Only God.*

But life knocks on the door of our hearts and, in a way, wakes us up to reality. So we set aside the things that allow us to feel God's pleasure. We have to focus on the nitty-gritty things of life to, well, keep life going. But I encourage you to remember to make time for the things that allow you to feel God's pleasure. Tap into them a little each day. Some days, get completely lost in them. Don't leave them on the sidelines, because they are the very things that put life into your daily dance.

Enjoying Your Design

We are each so uniquely wired that experiencing God's pleasure will look completely different from one person to the next. That's the beauty of it all. Our God created the landscape of the earth so vastly different from one state to the next, from one ocean to the next, from one galaxy to the next, and so has He created each of us so vastly different from one another. When we do the things we are designed to do and the things that give us great joy, it's like little specks of light going out into a dark world. And each of us doing our little sparkling dance together sends more and more light into this world. So be you. Pick up that paintbrush, gather those books, dive into that project, or rock motherhood . . . enjoy your design.

There are moments when I resist my design. One night at a Bible study, my leader looked me straight in the eyes and told me that I'm an empath; I take on the emotions of others and feel them too. But here's the catch: she pointed out that it was a gift and implored me to lean in to it. But, honestly, sometimes I wish I didn't feel so deeply because it can be exhausting. She helped me see that being an empath went hand in hand with being the kind of writer I longed to be. Maybe you wish you were more or less of something too—more studious, less serious, less passionate, more creative, less sensitive . . . you get the idea! But I encourage you to embrace your design.

We touched on this in chapter 2, but now I want to pinpoint how we easily resist our design instead of enjoying how we were created. This is because sometimes our design can look or feel like a weakness. But what if we instead viewed our perceived weaknesses as gifts? This doesn't mean we can't hope for growth or change in some areas. But often we resist the very way God made us—or at least I do. And living that way is frustrating. I don't know that I would write if I wasn't a feeler. What wouldn't you do if God had not wired you the way He did? The way you are wired points to the way you are gifted. Lean in to your design because God knew just what He was doing when He created you.

> The way you are wired points to the way you are gifted.

When You Want to Find Your Calling

We talked earlier about how God has dreams made just for us, and discovering those dreams are part of the dance of doing life with Him. I think sometimes we can get so hyperfocused on figuring out what our calling is—what God created us to do and be—that we lose the joy of the everyday.

Finding your calling is important, but right now I want to send some relief your way, because sometimes finding your calling can feel like a big mystery. It can feel confusing and exhausting, leaving you disappointed when it doesn't happen as quickly as you'd like. Dear dancing heart, you are called. Each of us is called to love God and to love others. God doesn't mean for your calling to be a big secret that only He knows and that you are constantly trying to figure out. Fulfilling your calling means pressing into your relationship with Jesus.

Sometimes we have to let go of giving our callings official titles and instead be fully confident in our Guide. God wants us to be so confident in who He is—in His faithful character and His heart for us—that we live life not just coasting through the grind but dancing with expectation and joy. Some of us know our callings, such as teacher, writer, dancer, or mom, while others of us are still trying to figure them out. And still others of us are discovering new callings by the decade. But we don't have to be in a web of confusion about this quest as long as we keep in step with our Savior day by day. He loves to dance with us through life, step-by-step. In some moments, we will question the direction we are going, and that's okay. In other moments, we will try something we thought God might be directing us toward only to discover it's not for us, and that's okay too. Part of the dance of dreaming with God and of savoring our dances is trying things. It's the trying, the conversations with the Lord, and the trusting Him with it all that makes life so purposeful!

> Fulfilling your calling means pressing into your relationship with Jesus.

He won't let us miss the things He has for us as long as we are seeking Him. While I do believe the enemy of our souls loves to distract and detour us from our callings, I also believe that as we seek Christ, He helps us stay connected to them. At times life may feel more like a battle than a dance. At other times, as we walk step-by-step with Him, we may feel things are gliding along pretty smoothly and we're staying on our toes. And still at other times we may feel like we're tripping over our own two feet. But in our stumbling, God carries us and redirects us. "Lord, you alone are my portion and my cup; you make my lot secure. The boundary lines have fallen for me in pleasant places; surely I have a delightful inheritance. I will praise the Lord, who counsels me" (Ps. 16:5–7).

God is our portion and our cup; He has assigned us just the right amount of what we need to do the things He wants to do through us. He has assigned us the correct qualifications, experiences, and personality and character traits we will need. He makes our callings—and, oh, there will be several over our lifetimes—completely secure. We don't have to chase them. We don't have to hold them with a fierce grip. We don't have to fear that someone will take them from us. They're secure because of His hold on them and His hold on us, just as our salvation in Him is secure.

God has put in place beautiful boundary lines that are good and pleasant. We think of boundaries as bad things sometimes, but we flourish within them. Boundary lines keep us in step with how God has designed us. This is a beautiful thing.

And our inheritance, all that we gain from knowing Jesus, all that He gifts us—complete forgiveness of all sin, grace to completely cover you—is delightful. When we keep His gifts in the forefront of our minds, we settle into the everyday steps of our callings with greater joy. And this: He counsels us. Think of the magnitude of this. The God of the universe counsels us.

You know, I think that's an invitation to sit down with Him and really have heart-to-hearts with Him on a daily basis. If we're caught up in confusion over our callings or the direction in our lives, we can pull up a chair to the heart of God. I recently came across Luke 3:21, which says, "As he was praying, heaven was opened." When Jesus pulled His heart up close to God's heart and prayed, heaven opened. While heaven is probably not going to literally open up when we pray, when we seek His counsel, He gladly opens His heart to us. He gladly gives us direction. He gladly offers us comfort. He gladly loves us right there in that moment. He gladly helps us find more clarity in our callings. He may not give us an outline and timeline of His plans, but He gladly provides us wisdom for the next step.

So when you feel your heart twisting into knots over His plans for you, get lost in something that makes your heart giddy. Get lost in those things that allow you to feel His pleasure. I say this with compassion because I know how hard it is to find time for those things. It can feel selfish to ignore the dirty dishes and dive into a good book instead. And clearly, you can't be lazy and drop all your responsibilities all the time. But when you do step away for a moment, you'll know when you need to get back to them. And the time away will be worth it, because your giddiness will help you enjoy your day-to-day responsibilities even more.

> o o o o o
>
> He may not give us an outline and timeline of His plans, but He gladly provides us wisdom for the next step.
>
> o o o o o

But when you leave out God's pleasure, your dance becomes a grind. Just like in marriage, as we talked about earlier, you have to be intentional about keeping the joy alive in your everyday life.

I typically danced two ways. One was an unjoyful way, caught up in the negative things. If I was caught up in the competition, the comparisons, the pressure, or the pain of injuries, dancing became a grind. Sometimes I wouldn't recognize it until I saw it in another dancer. It was as though they had lost the light in their eyes. But when I remembered what a blessing it was to dance, when I got lost in the character I was playing onstage, when I got caught up in the fun and forgot about the pressure, that's when dancing was truly joyful. And that's how I want to live life . . . dancing. Delighting in the good things, not caught up in the negative things. Living life dancing is really feeling God's pleasure. I invite you today to feel God's pleasure again by tuning in to the things He's instilled in you that make your heart dance with giddiness. I hope you're encouraged today to savor not only the big dream moments but also the everyday joys of life.

Prayer, Scripture, and Reflection
for Your Dreaming Heart

Jesus, bring the joy and giddiness back to my daily life, no matter where I am on my dreaming journey. Stir up my joy with Your love and the things that You wired my heart to enjoy. Show me how I can tap into those things each day and live life dancing. Help me savor the everyday pleasures and not just live for the big moments. May I see the delights of the everyday as I experience Your pleasure in the things You wired me to love. Ultimately, thank You for being my greatest source of joy and my constant Counselor through this dance of life.

_____

_____

_____

"For the joy of the LORD is your strength." Nehemiah 8:10

"The LORD is my strength and my shield; my heart trusts in him, and he helps me. My heart leaps for joy, and with my song I praise him." Psalm 28:7

"The LORD makes firm the steps of the one who delights in him." Psalm 37:23

_____

_____

_____

1. How is your level of joy in the day-to-day? Do you find yourself battling to find joy or does it come naturally to you?

_____

_____

_____

2. What makes you completely giddy? Have you considered that those things are your way of experiencing God's pleasure?

_____

_____

_____

3. If you were to give yourself permission to tap into those things today, what would that look like?

4. How does your giddiness for the things you love affect other areas of your life?

5. In what ways do you tend to resist your design? Which of your perceived weaknesses might actually be gifts?

6. How can you truly savor your dance today so you can live life dancing rather than living only for the big moments?

10

Standing with Intention,
Purpose, and Focus

Arise, go on your journey.

Deuteronomy 10:11 ESV

I write a lot about letting God lead this dance of life. Of course, that doesn't mean we don't work hard or set goals or live life with intention. So in this chapter we're going to go through what it looks like for us to live with intention, purpose, and focus while still letting God lead. It's one thing to dream with God, know what He has called us to do, and seek Him for wisdom, but it's a whole other thing to actually live out. Distractions, busyness, information overload, and discouragement can completely sideline us from living out God's plans for us.

Some of us thrive in setting goals and mapping out steps to reach those goals. Some of us wither instead because the goal setting is just too overwhelming. We all function differently and must discover how we best function when it comes to intentionally living out God's dance for us. So whether you scribble notes on the pages of this chapter, fill out the goal sheets in your cute day planner, or create reminders in your iPhone, I invite you to get purposeful. A million things pull at us for attention. To dance through life well, we need to be intentional.

While onstage, a dancer lets muscle memory take over. She becomes lost in the movement and joy of dancing. But being able to perform so smoothly doesn't just happen; it's the result of careful intentionality. She has to think through each step and every movement. She has to deflect bad habits. She has to dance with thoughtfulness and care to make her movements look effortless.

○ ○ ○ ○ ○

To dance through life well, we need to be intentional.

○ ○ ○ ○ ○

She has to tune out worries and cares to grow and focus. She has to remember that every rehearsal matters. She has to remember that all the work behind the scenes is worth it. She has to remember *why* she dances. She has to believe her dancing matters. She has to trust it's making an impact. Sometimes she will not know if her dancing has made an impact until the curtain goes down and an audience member hugs her neck.

She can't just casually go about her training. It takes effort, energy, and enthusiasm. There's a beautiful balance of knowing when to work and when to rest. Staying in that balance keeps her dancing, and valuing what she does keeps her excited. In the same way, we must be careful and intentional about how we spend our time, our days, and therefore our lives so that we stay in touch with God and His plans for us.

Valuing Your Place in This World

A beautiful place to start in living life with intention, purpose, and focus is by valuing our place in this world, understanding that

God has specific purposes for us. I know that sometimes it feels like if we are not doing something big and impactful or if we are unknown and not famous, our lives aren't all that valuable. Now that we have the world at our fingertips through our phones and social media and easy access to the world of celebrities and such, if we are not careful, our hearts can begin to believe a lie that says our quiet lives are insignificant. We can easily lose sight of the precious value of our lives.

When I looked up the definition of *value*, I found words like *regard, esteem highly, worth, merit, importance*. Have you seen your life, your work, your dreams, your everyday activities as really important lately? Have you seen these things as highly valuable?

Sometimes you just need a little nudge of encouragement to assure you that what you do matters and is worth being intentional and focused about. When you lose sight of the value of your place in the world, you lose the motivation to live out your callings with confidence and enthusiasm.

Often you don't see a return on your work. You don't know if it's impacted anyone. You don't see yourself as making a difference in the world. But God sees. He sees what no one else can. Your work, even though you don't always recognize its value, is indispensable to God.

I save every card from my husband, every hand-drawn note from my boys, and every letter from my readers. They're little gifts to remind me that what I do is valuable to God. And every so often, when no notes, no cards come, those are the times when I exercise a little more faith—faith that God sees the value of my life.

Nothing can really measure the value of what you do. So as a starting place to living with intention, purpose, and focus, I encourage you to take note of why your life is significant. I want you to see the importance of what you do and that it really matters. It impacts others, it gives you joy, it allows you to feel God's pleasure, and it puts much-needed light into the world. Challenge yourself to think through why you do what you do. How is it helping others? How is it pointing to God? How is it delighting God? How is it delighting you?

So instead of setting mile-high goals, start with the why behind them. Why do they matter? Why are they important to you? Starting there will help you find strong footing for standing with intention, purpose, and focus.

Looking Up for Inspiration

Next, look up for inspiration. This is slightly different from what we talked about earlier, regarding staying inspired. Our tendency is to look around. But God is the creator of creativity, and when we look to Him for inspiration, help, and guidance, our creativity flourishes. Creativity flourishes with space and time and slow moments of living. It's important to turn off the noise, shut down the phone, and spend some time looking to God for inspiration in our dreams and our daily lives.

o o o o o

When we unravel ourselves from the world and wind back up into the arms and presence of God, we find our focus.

o o o o o

One thing I loved about stepping into a ballet studio is that dancing was the only thing I could really think about when I was there. If I started daydreaming about to-do lists or other things, I was likely to bump into another dancer or slip and fall. It usually took me until ronds de jambe, that's about halfway through the barre exercises, to completely let go of my real-life thoughts and focus on all things ballet. I enjoyed slowly letting go of all the distractions and tuning in to my dancing.

Likewise, keeping a single focus is important when we're looking for inspiration. In an age of the internet, it's hard to completely turn off all the noise and to focus. But what might we find if we turn it all off and simply look to God for inspiration? When we unravel ourselves from the world and wind back up into the arms and presence of God, we find our focus.

On a writing day, if I don't completely turn off my phone, I cannot find my inspiration. I'm distracted by too many things—good things—but the writing doesn't happen. There's a freedom in turning off the noise and looking up for inspiration. Turning off the noise gives us a chance to hear God's whispers. His whispers are where we find our greatest source of inspiration for all we do. I love these verses in Isaiah 48: "Come near me and listen . . . I am the LORD your God, who teaches you what is best for you, who directs you in the way you should go" (vv. 16–17). He longs for us to hear Him and for us to focus on doing the things He has called us to do.

> Turning off the noise gives us a chance to hear God's whispers.

Just as a dancer gets to the studio and tunes out the rest of the world to focus on her dancing, I invite you today to tune out the world for a while and completely plug into God. That's where you'll find inspiration for your dreams and your daily life. It will take some time to completely unravel from the noise and chatter, but it will be worth the effort.

Progress over Perfection

"Just make a dent." That's what Brian says to me when I tell him I'm going to work on a writing project. Sometimes I get all gung ho that I'm going to finish my project or write x number of words. In the face of my enthusiasm, he gently reminds me to just make a little bit of progress at a time. I tend to want to accomplish an entire project at once, but when I do, I quickly become overwhelmed by the enormity of it. But giving myself the freedom to just make a dent keeps me from becoming overwhelmed, feeling inadequate, and completely burning out.

When it comes to making progress toward the goals and dreams God has given us, there is wisdom in pacing ourselves and embracing progress over perfection. This goes back a little bit to what we talked about earlier—taking time to play, have fun, and enjoy life. If we're constantly working only on our goals or our dreams, we can easily exhaust ourselves. We need a change of scenery. A mom, for example, sometimes just needs a little time alone. A dancer sometimes just needs to do something not related to dancing. A writer sometimes just needs to put down her pen.

So as you dream with God and work out some goals with Him, I encourage you to "just make a dent." Set realistic expectations. Don't try to change everything today. Don't try to master all your goals at once. Leave plenty of white space on the calendar and time to just be, to live, to laugh, and to have fun. See every little dent of progress as valuable. Sometimes when we set the bar too high, we give up in frustration.

> We can always trust in His unwavering, guiding lead.

I think that's the sweetest part of dreaming with God—the beautiful rest we experience in knowing He has our back. With God, we have a Helper. With God, we're not left to do life on our own. God is the keeper of time, and He is never in a rush. Our time is in His able hands, and He will nudge us when maybe we need to hurry up a bit. He will also tug on our hearts when we need to slow down a bit. We can always trust in His unwavering, guiding lead.

Turn, Remember, Hold Fast, Start

This chapter makes me think about the journey the Israelites endured to the Promised Land. It was a land they longed for and could hardly wait to experience. They wanted something new, fresh, and good. We all long for that in life. We all long for new land in the landscape of our own lives. The following verses from Deuteronomy stick out to me as we press toward a life of beautiful intention, purpose, and focus:

> You have stayed long enough at this mountain. Turn and take your journey, and go. . . . See, I have set the land before you. Go in and take possession of the land. (Deut. 1:6–8 ESV)

These words can provide us with inspiration to turn, step into a new journey, and go. This journey of dreaming with God and tuning in to His presence in your life is pointing you and me to something new. A new land. A new dance. A deeper connection with the Lord. One of purpose. One that requires focus on the Lord. One that takes intention. Many times throughout Scripture, God reminds us, "Do not fear or be dismayed" (Deut. 1:21 ESV). It can be daunting and hard to try something new. But He implores us not to fear or get tangled up inside. He's got us in this new thing.

The theme of remembering God runs throughout Deuteronomy.

> Do not be in dread or afraid of them. The LORD your God who goes before you will himself fight for you, just as he did for you in Egypt before your eyes, and in the wilderness, where you have seen how the LORD your God carried you, as a man carries his son, all the way that you went until you came to this place. (Deut. 1:29–31 ESV)

Our journeys with the Lord require us to remember how He has been faithful in Scripture and in our lives. Scripture points us to His faithfulness, grace, and love. And our journeys remind us of the times He has come through for us. It's vital for us to remember our personal history with the Lord. There will be mountain moments and valley moments and all things in between, but reflecting on our relationship with Him gives us a sense of calm about the land He is bringing us to.

That's why I love to journal. My journals are my history books of my relationship with the Lord. When I need a reminder that God's in control, that He sees me, and that He's got me and my whole dance of life, I dive into an old journal. When we reflect on our history with Him, new courage for the paths ahead takes hold of us and we step into new territory with stronger confidence in Him.

Deuteronomy 11:22 says, "Loving the Lord your God, walking in all his ways, and holding fast to him" (ESV). This verse says it all. Our journeys are about loving God, walking in His ways, and holding on to Him. But here's the thing: He's also holding on to us! God goes into our lives ahead of us. He already sees our steps. He already knows what's ahead. In His all-knowingness, He also goes with us. As much as He is ahead of us, working and establishing the steps forward, He walks side by side with us throughout our journeys. Holding out His hand, He gently whispers, "I got you." And onward we go into a new land or dance that He has set before us.

Can we talk about *Dancing with the Stars* for a moment? In a short recorded clip before Laurie and Val danced one night in the 2016 season, the show featured a performance of the two gliding across the floor together, and Val, while holding Laurie and spinning her around the corner, whispered, "I got you." Laurie had just lost her grandmother. It was an emotional night for her, to say the least. Her partner carried her through the performance and his "I got you" completely got me. It was precious and beautiful. It resonated so deeply with me because an "I got you" from someone we love and someone who loves us is one of the best things in the world.

> There will be mountain moments and valley moments and all things in between, but reflecting on our relationship with Him gives us a sense of calm about the land He is bringing us to.

To know someone has our back and cares so deeply for us is to know great strength and new courage. This makes me think of Brian's pep talks when I'm discouraged or overwhelmed in my writing. Right when I think I can't continue, he picks me up and, in his own way, tells me that he's got me. He's with me. He's for me. He believes in me. And great strength and new courage rise up in my heart.

To know someone is there for us makes us brave. The love they show through their support points us back to the right path when we've lost our way. An "I got you" gives us the boost we need to keep dreaming with God.

When God whispers, "I got you," you become brave. When the journey grows discouraging, and it will at times, pause to remind your soul, "He's got me." And keep holding fast to Him.

Hope for Fresh Beginnings

My family has a small space in the corner of our backyard that I like to call our little rose garden. We fenced it off to keep Shaka, our puppy, out of it. He loved to get in there and "help" trim my hyacinth bean plant and rosebushes. We also pulled out some overgrown purple salvia, much to my heart's dismay. I love lavender-colored flowers of any type, so pulling them out was a little sad, but they were taking over the garden to the point that we couldn't see any roses.

After our little renovation, Brian and I stood back and admired our freshly weeded, trimmed down, and protected little garden. It looked simplified, spacious, and tidy. As the weeks went by and the sun hit the roses just right, it was as if it were pulling them out of an invisible shell. They began to stand taller and reach toward the sun; they started to fill out, blossom, and bloom. It was fascinating to watch them grow, and we quickly realized they were thriving because they had room to grow. And not to mention, they didn't have a little puppy constantly taste testing them.

In our everyday lives, sin is a lot like that overgrown salvia Brian and I pulled from our rose garden. It invades our lives, choking the life right out of us.

And here's the thing: sin can be subtle. It can feel very not sin-like. Good things and good desires, just like my purple salvia, can take over and consume our hearts—and that's the point at which they become a problem. Sin can hide and crowd the gifts and callings God has instilled in us. That's why keeping the Lord in our dancing through life is so vital. In His love and sweetness, He points out things that need to go. He points out things that are suppressing His light in us. This makes me think about artistic directors and choreographers. While it's not always fun to be told that my steps are a little off, they see the bigger picture. When I apply their corrections, my dancing improves.

○ ○ ○ ○ ○

Sin can be subtle.

○ ○ ○ ○ ○

New life and hope for fresh beginnings are waiting to bloom under the weeds of sin. And God wants us to find these hidden treasures. He wants us to discover all the precious talents, abilities, and gifts He instilled in us that have been crowded out. But we have to find the weeds first and, with His help, pull them from our lives.

When we take the time to really examine our lives and recognize the sins that are choking the life right out of us, we, like the roses,

Begin to stand taller.

Begin to reach toward the Son.

Begin to blossom and bloom.

God wants us to be free from sin to do our kingdom work.

Let us throw off everything that hinders and the sin that so easily entangles. And let us run with perseverance the race marked out for us. (Heb. 12:1)

We have races to run, people to love, work to do, dances to dance, growth and blossoming ahead, but we must release all the entanglements. The doubt. The fear. The insecurity. The comparing. The worrying about what people think. All of it.

What a gracious God we have who loves for us to flourish for His kingdom purposes. And here is the sweetest news: His grace covers us. Wherever you are, wherever you've been, or whatever sin is overgrowing in your heart, God sees you through the lenses of grace and forgiveness. He will gladly take your hand and help you step out of the weeds and into new freedom.

Prayer, Scripture, and Reflection
for Your Dreaming Heart

Thank You, Lord, for inviting me to dance through life with You and for showing me that it will take intention, purpose, and focus. Help me hold fast and draw close to You for wisdom and direction. Thank You for staying with me every step of the journey and for faithfully leading me through life thus far. Show me the weeds that are crowding You out and that need to go. I praise You for Your constant hold on me and Your guidance in helping me flourish.

"But be assured today that the LORD your God is the one who goes across ahead of you like a devouring fire." Deuteronomy 9:3

"Arise, go on your journey." Deuteronomy 10:11 ESV

"Come to the rest and to the inheritance that the LORD your God is giving you." Deuteronomy 12:9 ESV

"The Mighty One has done great things for me—holy is his name." Luke 1:49

_____

_____

_____

_____

_____

1. Why is your work valuable to God?

_____

_____

_____

2. Where do you typically look for inspiration and how can you intentionally look up to God today for inspiration?

_____

_____

_____

3. How can you make "just a dent" in the work God has led you to do today?

4. How has your history with God encouraged you?

5. In what ways do you need to tend your soul today?

11

∘∘∘∘∘∘∘∘∘∘∘∘∘∘∘∘∘∘∘∘∘∘∘

Seeking God When Your Dreams Don't Come True

My grace is sufficient for you, for my power is made
perfect in weakness.

2 Corinthians 12:9

We can't talk about dreaming with God without discussing
what to do when our dreams don't come true. What do
we do when our life plans don't work out the way we thought they
would or even the way we thought God wanted them to? What
do we do when we feel like somehow God has left us in the dark?

I know we touched on this a little bit back in chapter 4, but
I want to take it a step further in this chapter. The hardest part
about trusting God with the dreams of our hearts is understanding
that every dream we dream isn't necessarily going to come true. In
fact, dreaming with God is risky heart business. Some of you have
been completely sideswiped by life. Maybe one of your dreams

has completely fallen through. Maybe you've experienced deep loss. Maybe the life you had been standing on has been completely swept away. Maybe you are frustrated by the lot God has chosen for you. Maybe you want something different—or you think you want something different. Maybe you've been praying for a dream and it's just not happening. Maybe it's clear it's never going to happen.

We're just going to sit in that tension a bit here in this chapter because we've all experienced some disappointment, hurt, or loss in regard to the dreams of our hearts. And we must acknowledge this. We must look to God for comfort. We must feel the weight in order to feel the hope of God, the peace of God, and the presence of God. We're going to talk about the detours, delays, and dreams that don't come true, as well as the invitation to seek God through it all instead of defaulting to despair, discouragement, or even dancing out of step with God's plans for us.

The Greatest Example

The greatest example we can turn to is Jesus's life. His life, His dance with God, was anything but roses and butterflies. But He lived with deep joy and sweet contentment, never in a hurry, always stopping to love somebody. He did His work with enthusiasm and peace. He never fretted over the future or analyzed the past. His dance included possibly the most excruciating pain known to humankind—crucifixion. He agonized in prayer to God over the "whys" of having to face the cross. He felt left in the dark. He felt maybe even abandoned by God. Only God, His Father, could see the beauty that the ashes would bring. Jesus's pain became our greatest deliverance, our pathway to eternal joy. His dance of life became the heartbeat to our dances through life.

> His dance of life became the heartbeat to our dances through life.

146

His dream of doing God's work included hard moments, deep valleys, and dark nights. But He pressed on and trusted God's heart. He trusted God's love. All He wanted to do was "be about [His] Father's business" (Luke 2:49 KJV). His dance was entirely about His Father's business. That's what He lived and loved for. While knowing Christ endured hard valleys in life doesn't fix our pain, it's comforting to know He understands it completely.

Jesus's greatest pain became His greatest mission. His pain became our gain. And God will use your pain to be your greatest mission. He will use your pain to help someone else. You will be able to use your pain and lost dreams to help and encourage someone, to put light into someone else's life.

I penned the following in my journal a while back when I was feeling the tension of dreams delayed and detoured.

If I wasn't weak, I wouldn't know His strength.

If everything in my life was perfect, I wouldn't know the power of prayer.

If I didn't need Him, I would never know His love.

If I was always confident, bold, and strong, I would never need to ask God for help.

If I never knew tears, I would never know He's the One who can wipe them away.

If I never had a tough day, I would never rejoice in the good ones.

If I never knew fatigue, I would never know His power.

If I always knew just what to say, I would never need His Spirit.

If I always knew what step to take next, I would never need the Helper.

If I always felt at peace, I would never experience His healing.

If I knew exactly what to do with my life, I would never know His direction for what I was made for.

If I never ached for a dream to come true, I would never know that nothing is impossible for God.

If I knew all the answers, I would never know the delight of His Word.

If my ballet technique had been perfect, I would have never known the reward of hard work.

If parenting and marriage were easy, I would have never surrendered them to God.

If I weren't a tiny bit on the emotional and introspective side, I would never need time in my Savior's presence, and I would miss out on knowing His love and grace.

You see, we all wish our weaknesses and hard moments away. But without them, we wouldn't need a relationship with Him.

What about you? What in your life has pointed you to God? To a closer relationship with Him? There were times, especially on this writing road, when I ran into one detour or delay after another. But I've learned that detours and delays often redirect us back to God.

His detours often become points of reflection, of evaluating and examining our lives before Him. Delays lead us to press into Him. Both become springboards to a deeper walk with Him. I'm not saying I love detours and delays or that they are easy by any means, but just acknowledging that they're part of dreaming with God is important to our journeys. We'll also experience moments of disappointment along our dreaming journeys. But as we embrace His love for us, we begin to see that often the disappointments are part of the detours; they lead to the beautiful flow of God's direction for our lives and a deeper relationship with Him in which we completely depend on Him.

> Detours and delays often redirect us back to God.

Beauty in Dependence

Our human nature is to do life without God. Sometimes it feels easier to do what we want to do the way we want to do it. It's simpler to just make things happen, whatever the cost. But there's beauty in dependence on the Lord. When we depend on God, we live differently.

Dancing with the Lord through life isn't necessarily about fulfilling our dreams; it's about deepening our dependence on Him. When dreams don't come true, we can count on the One who guides us. The detours, delays, and disappointments become signposts to point the way to Him.

> When we depend on God, we live differently.

I love this definition of *depend*: "to rely for support, maintenance, help."[1] In our dependence on God, we can rely on Him fully for support, heart maintenance, and help. Don't we all need heart maintenance sometimes? I know I do! When dreams fall through, when delays and detours bombard us, when disappointments envelop us, we can always run to the Lord for heart maintenance.

Just as our natural inclination is to default to despair when things aren't turning out the way we want, we can easily default to plans of our own instead of seeking God for His plans for us. Opportunities come at us and ideas grow inside us, but how many of us tend to go for them now and pray about them later? We jump into things before we consult the Lord. I can be a jumper for sure. Sometimes I go after an opportunity or open door before I talk to God about it. I jump, I leap, and then at some point I become stressed. I realize I defaulted to saying yes without seeking God's best for me. I long for my default mode to be one that seeks God first, above everything else. Sometimes it may seem unproductive

1. Dictionary.com, s.v. "depend," accessed June 15, 2017, http://www.dictionary.com/browse/depend?s=t.

or silly or like a waste of time to slow down to earnestly seek God in a situation. But it's in the slowing down and the seeking that we find divine direction, clarity, and wisdom.

Dreaming with God Is Worth It

God makes things good and right. According to Isaiah 40:4, "The crooked shall be made straight, and the rough places plain" (KJV). In those moments when our dreams slide downhill, we can know that when the Word of God is in our hearts, our steps will not slide (see Ps. 37:31). Our Father in heaven sees all our troubles, loves us through them all, and recognizes the grand picture of the dance of our lives. I'm not going to say we should sweep our troubles under the rug or that everything's going to be okay or that we should simply move on. No, sometimes we will need to accept that it's okay to feel hurt and disappointment. And when we do, we can find comfort in the Lord.

> It's in the slowing down and the seeking that we find divine direction, clarity, and wisdom.

When we feel we're in the dark and wonder what the next step is, we can always know that the best move is to seek the Lord. All of us have experienced hard things. We all know the hurt of a dream that's gone downhill. How we react comes down to our theology. Our theology is what we believe about God. If we believe God is good, then our hearts will rest in where we are in our dreaming journeys. If we believe He is at work, then we'll know deep down that our dreaming journeys will work out in more beautiful ways than we ever could imagine. Sometimes it's just really hard to get our hearts in line with our theology. While we'll always have to sit in that tension of not knowing how our dreams will work out, we can always know God is leading.

One thing I'm sure of is that the truth of God's Word is God's love language right straight to our hearts. Our hearts are designed to hear the Word, to know the truth, and to find hope in His divine Word. We need the Word of God. It speaks to our hearts in ways human words can't.

> My soul is weary with sorrow;
> strengthen me according to your word. (Ps. 119:28)

Ultimately, God's Word is the strongest foundation for our dreaming journeys and our lives. When dreams collide, crash, or completely dissolve, God's Word still stands. He has truths and words just for our dreaming hearts. His Word settles us like nothing else can. These hearts of ours, they can feel like untamed horses—wild and jumpy and restless. His Word meets us in our restlessness and calms our storms. It's a direct line to His heart. And combining His Word with prayer keeps our hearts in rhythm with His heart.

> While we'll always have to sit in that tension of not knowing how our dreams will work out, we can always know God is leading.

Sometimes dreams are simply not going to come true. But despite that reality, we know God still reigns in our lives. And the intimacy we find with God along the way makes dreaming worth the disappointments. The giddiness, the joy, the impossibilities, the hope, and the fun make dreaming with God worth it all.

Those you and God moments of heart maintenance are what it's all about. Press into the Lord, sweet one. Know that He has your delays, your detours, and your disappointments. He knows them. He has you. Just be held by Him in those moments. Just be held.

Dreams Come True and Dreams Come Undone

My sister Katie and her husband, Reece, struggled with infertility for three years. Although I could see the hurt and questions in Katie's eyes throughout the struggle, she never complained. She just kept praying. My siblings and I had a growing crew of kiddos—all boys. Brian and I have three boys, my oldest brother and sister-in-law have three boys, and my other brother and sister-in law have five. Count 'em, five! And the youngest are twin boys. So my parents have eleven grandsons. I often lose track of how many nephews I have. My sweet sister quietly trusted God with her dream for a baby—and it wasn't happening. I struggled to know how to encourage her. Half of me wanted to spur her on and assure her that the Lord would be faithful and His timing would be perfect. But the other half of me questioned if I would be giving her false hope. None of us knew if they would be able to have a baby. So I tried to hug her a lot. And all of us prayed. I can't imagine Katie and Reece's angst and even grief over what may never come. Having a baby was a dream that I'm sure felt delayed, on hold, and even completely impossible at times.

But they continued to pray. They continued to pray not so much for a baby, but for God's very best for them. They continued to believe that His plans for them were not just good, but amazing. The way they quietly pressed into the Lord during this time ministered to me and to many others.

Typically, when someone in my family announces they are expecting a baby, we get all kinds of loud and dramatic. There's lots of screaming, jumping up and down, and hugging, and the happy couple tells the big story of how it all came about. Those baby announcements are some of my favorite memories with my family.

So when Katie announced that she and Reece were finally expecting, she was anticipating a full-on dance and screaming party. But on that beautiful summer evening in Crested Butte, Colorado, with our entire family gathered around a dinner table at our favorite Mexican restaurant for my dad's birthday (well, we had two tables . . . the eleven grandsons had their own), no one danced or screamed. Instead, we were all speechless and teary. We all kind of stared at her and Reece, totally stunned. Stunned by God. Stunned by His timing. Stunned by their continual faith in Him. She was probably a little disappointed by our initial reactions, but after the shock wore off, we laughed and hugged and squealed. Then we all stayed up way too late dreaming about this precious little gem who was getting ready to make their way into the world. And we basked in God's faithfulness.

The story gets even sweeter. Further into Katie's pregnancy, when it was time for them to reveal the gender of the baby, my entire family gathered at my parents' house for the big reveal. We all held a balloon with a color representing what gender we thought the baby would be—pink for a girl or blue for a boy. There was a good mixture of guesses. Would it be the twelfth grandson or the first granddaughter?

Reece and Katie had a big box sealed up with balloons inside, and when they opened the box, a mass of pink balloons floated out. All I remember is Katie jumping up and down and all of us screaming. Pure joy. Pure faithfulness of God. Pure sweetness of God. Not that we wouldn't have been excited if it was a boy, but it was so sweet that God gave Katie and Reece the first (and currently the only) baby girl after all they had been through.

And Reece and Katie's little girl, who is now almost one, is a constant reminder that God hears. He's good. He's faithful.

When our dreams don't come true or when they seem completely impossible, we can turn to the Lord and trust His ways. My heart hurts for those of you who are experiencing a dream undone right now. I want to say all the right things and encourage you in the right way, but all I know is that I don't know the answers. However, I'm inspired by the way Katie and Reece sought the Lord when they felt hopeless. And I think stories like theirs remind us to do the same when our dreams threaten to undo us. We all will have dreams that don't come true. We all will experience long waits,

Dreaming with God

seemingly unanswered prayers, and heartache. These things are part of our journey of dreaming with God.

But remember that God knows our every desire and dream. He knows our fear and pain and disappointment. If God feels about us the way I felt about watching my baby sister wait and wonder about God's plans for her, He is the sweetest God. He takes on your pain, waiting, and unfulfilled dreams. He feels the weight of these things along with you. He may not always make your dreams come true, but He will help you walk through the heartbreak.

There's this little gem of a verse in Luke 1 that says, "Your prayer has been heard" (v. 13). An angel of the Lord said this to Zechariah upon giving him the news that his prayers for a child had been heard and God had faithfully answered them.

Whatever prayer requests you have been bringing to God, know that He hears you. He hears every single request. Every cry, every appeal, every wish for others, every prayer for help with the habits and hang-ups of your heart, for big dreams and practical things . . . all of it. He hears. It takes faith to believe that He hears. Sometimes you may feel like you're throwing out prayers but not seeing any evidence that God hears them. Know that as you journey through this dance of life, God hears. Keep praying in faith.

It's in the praying that we find God's peace. While we may still want answers, His peace is immeasurable. We can know His peace even when we don't have His answers or when we don't like His answers. But through our praying and seeking, we discover He's faithful, always listening, and always in control. He carries us. He holds us. He's our strong foundation when the foundations of our dreams crumble.

So why keep dreaming, hoping, and praying when dreams sometimes don't come true? Because this life is a mixture of dreams come true and dreams undone, and seeking God in and through it is where we find the comfort and healing we need for our dream-hungry hearts throughout the journey.

154

While I wish every dream came true, I'm thankful we have the God of the universe to walk us through the dreams undone. While the journey isn't fun or pretty or easy, He keeps our souls dancing when they feel like calling it quits. We can still get mad, sad, and frustrated when life doesn't go our way. It's okay to feel those things. But we have Someone we can bring all those feelings to. He meets us where we are. He tends to our hearts. He ministers to our souls.

Whether dreams come true or dreams come undone, we have a constant Source, an ever-present Encourager, and One who continues to pick us up. I'm so thankful we have a Savior who jumps up and down with us and delights with us when dreams come true and who holds us and carries us when dreams come undone. Keep pressing into the Lord, sweet one.

> ○ ○ ○ ○ ○
>
> This life is a mixture of dreams come true and dreams undone, and seeking God in and through it is where we find the comfort and healing we need for our dream-hungry hearts throughout the journey.
>
> ○ ○ ○ ○ ○

Prayer, Scripture, and Reflection
for Your Dreaming Heart

Lord, You know the delays, detours, and disappointments in my own dreaming journey. You know every single one. Thank You that I can run to You when I feel the tension and weight of those things. Thank You that Your Word

*constantly points me in the right direction and that You
are shaping me and guiding me through every delay and
detour. Give me a hunger to know You in a deeper way, to
seek You, and to trust Your ways. Give me confident faith
in who You are and in Your faithfulness. When my dreams
don't come true, may I confidently step toward You and
desperately depend on You. Thank You for meeting me at
every stop and in every dark place. Thank You for being
the light of my life. Thank You that Your grace and Your
presence are enough for me in my own dance through life.
You are all I need.*

"Your word, LORD, is eternal; it stands firm in the heavens. Your faithfulness continues through all generations." Psalm 119:89–90

"I am your servant; give me discernment that I may understand your statutes." Psalm 119:125

"The unfolding of your words gives light; it gives understanding to the simple." Psalm 119:130

"Direct my footsteps according to your word." Psalm 119:133

_____

_____

_____

1. When in your life have you felt like you landed in a detour, delay, or disappointment in regard to the dreams of your heart?

_____

_____

_____

2. When a dream falls through, what is your default mode? To go and make it happen? To seek the Lord? To do something else?

_____

_____

_____

3. Describe a time when your pain became a pathway to drawing closer to the Lord or a time when good came out of a bad situation.

_____

_____

_____

4. How might your heart need some maintenance in the Lord today? What things need realignment? What truths need reinforcing?

_____

_____

_____

5. What will you choose to believe about God when your dreams fall through?

_____

_____

_____

12

∘ ∘

Stepping into the Sweetest Dance

He will not let your foot slip—he who watches over
you will not slumber.

Psalm 121:3

Any dancer, whether she is a professional ballerina or a novice
learning the two-step, first has to learn the steps before she
soaks in the entire dance. Then the dance becomes ingrained into
her mind and muscles so deeply that she arrives at a place where
she can dance freely, not thinking so much about the steps. The
dancer in me wants each of us to close this book knowing the
steps, counts, and exact positions of our own dreaming dances
with God so we can dance and live freely, not having to think so
much about the steps. But there's no perfect formula of steps in
our dreaming with God. We have journeyed together to discover
that the whole point of dreaming with God is to know Him and
to help others know Him. In this final chapter, I want to encourage
you to step into and stand strong in God's sweetest dance for you.

Standing Strong

How a ballet dancer stands is everything when it comes to dancing. A dancer spends years perfecting how she stands because it affects her technique. A dancer is trained to stand tall, abdominals engaged, shoulders down, neck long, and body strong. I used to always tell my ballet students that the strength of their posture, how they stand, takes them immediately from looking like a student to looking like a professional. Standing tall and strong is powerful. And when we dream with God, we have to stand strong with Him against the ways of our culture. Culture will try to convince us to take our dreams and matters into our own hands. Dreaming with God means standing tall and staying solid in His ways.

This dreaming thing is tricky because faith doesn't say to sit on our couches and do nothing, nor does it say go make our dreams come true all on our own. But as we've talked about in the pages of this book, the secret lies in seeking Christ. He will walk us through step by step, by step, by step, and in the stepping we slowly become the women God dreamt up.

> He will walk us through step by step, by step, by step, and in the stepping we slowly become the women God dreamt up.

When we leave God out of our dreaming, we are truly missing out on the adventure He has planned for us—the one that fits us like Cinderella's slipper, the one we are made for, the one our gifts and skills are tailored to, the one that truly delights us. He has more joy, more peace, more excitement, more life for us if we will invite Him to come along on the adventure. And don't just invite Him—let Him lead.

We have a real enemy who does not want us to dream with God. In fact, he tries to make us fall. He'll do everything he can to get us to a place where we give up on God and start following our own path and our own ways:

There is a way that seems right to a man,
but its end is the way to death. (Prov. 14:12 ESV)

That verse is what Satan wants to get us to stand on, the way that seems right to us. Our plans, our dreams, our ways of following our dreams. So Satan, our very real and powerful enemy, will keep up with his subtle schemes to convince us that following after our dreams in our own strength is the way to success. He does not want us to lean on God in any way, shape, or form because he knows that when we do, we will blossom into women who impact others for Christ and overflow with abundant life. He knows we will be joyful and happy seeking Christ, and to him that's dangerous. His subtle schemes keep us from standing on the truth that God's way is best. He uses comparison, distraction, and busyness to convince us we don't need God. That's his way, to sneak in and slowly make us feel troubled, discouraged, and defeated in our dreams.

I easily forget about Satan's influence. When my children ask about him, I tend to make him out to be an evil bad guy with red horns, something they would see in their superhero books. I don't want to scare them. It's a strange, creepy thought that he is out there, manipulating, discouraging, destroying. But then again, I want my kiddos to know he is dangerous. I want Brian and me to be aware of his influence in our lives. I want to remember he's out there trying to get me off God's path for me. And I want you to know he's prowling around.

Be alert and of sober mind. Your enemy the devil prowls around like a roaring lion looking for someone to devour. (1 Pet. 5:8)

For our struggle is not against flesh and blood, but against the rulers, against the authorities, against the powers of this dark world and against the spiritual forces of evil in the heavenly realms. (Eph. 6:12)

Knowing this, being aware of Satan's subtle schemes, we can be on alert. As much as we would rather not linger on the thought that Satan is at work around us trying to trip us up, it's good to remember that not-so-fun truth so we lean in to God more than ever. Thankfully, our God and Savior is stronger and more powerful than he is. Between Satan's influence and culture's messages, dreaming with God will easily lose its appeal if we aren't careful. All the things we have talked about throughout these chapters keep us standing strong in our dances with God through life.

The Only True Fulfillment

I know the world advertises big, luxurious dreams and that once you reach your dreams, you'll finally feel fulfilled. I have felt those messages too. But I want to share one last story that has grabbed my heart.

Recently, Brian and I were flying to California (we love that state!). He was taking me to see American Ballet Theater's production of *The Nutcracker*. I was a teeny bit excited! I'm thirty-seven years old but still turn into a ten-year-old when it comes to attending the ballet. We got situated in our seats on the plane and much to my heart's delight, we saw that each passenger had their own movie screen to watch any movie of their choosing. If this is old news, clearly we don't fly much. Like we were kiddos again, we each began searching for the perfect movie to watch during the flight. I went straight to the romantic comedies and documentaries. Brian went straight to the science fiction and action movies. Of course, the first documentary I came across was about a ballet dancer. *Score!*

As we soared through the sky, I took in the story of a ballet dancer's journey to stardom. He reached the pinnacle of every young aspiring dancer's dreams and became a principal dancer of one of the greatest ballet companies in the world. But his story was so intriguing and heartbreaking because once he reached his dream, it wasn't enough. He lit up the stage every evening before thousands and received standing ovations, but at the end of the day, he went home to an empty apartment and an empty heart. Despite everything he had accomplished in his dance career, he still felt unfulfilled. Fame didn't satisfy. Success didn't satisfy. Being at the top of his profession didn't satisfy. As our plane landed in California, it dawned on me how I wanted to land this book.

Don't believe the world's lie that once you accomplish your dreams, your heart will forever be fulfilled. Place your need for fulfillment in the only One who can truly fulfill your heart.

> Place your need for fulfillment in the only One who can truly fulfill your heart.

When you place your significance, purpose, and identity in Jesus, the dreams you live out become experiences to deepen your intimacy with Him instead of temporary fixes for an empty heart. He wants us to dream with Him, but He longs to be our greatest dream come true. Our dreams will give us sweet satisfaction and a sense of fulfillment when He's our true source of sustaining fulfillment. Because of Jesus, we get to do a different kind of dreaming dance. Instead of stressing and striving, we are offered the opportunity to pray and lean on Christ and therefore find a deeper satisfaction than the world can offer.

Begin Your Dance

So begin your dance of dreaming with God, but remember to let the journey and your relationship with God be the sweet part. I encourage you to step into God's sweetest dance for you by surrendering every dream and desire of your heart to the One who knows you best and knows what is best for you. You can tell Him all your crazy ideas and He will gladly direct your steps. Sometimes you will try something and quickly realize it's not for you. Sometimes you will step into a dream and find out it's much more difficult than you had imagined, but God will gladly give you the strength you need to keep going. And sometimes you will feel like one of your dreams will never happen or is just plain silly, but God has a beautiful way of surprising us when we surrender completely to Him. Be willing to let God work out the details of your dreams. Be willing to take your hands off the situation and faithfully do the things that are right in front of you. Trust that God is at work behind the scenes for you. Watch what He does. Trust Him to open doors that seem locked shut. Trust Him to close doors that are better off shut. Trust Him with every step of your dreaming journey and remember He is with you in all of it. Keep your eyes on Jesus and dance confidently in the direction of the dreams God gives you.

> o o o o o
>
> Keep your eyes on Jesus and dance confidently in the direction of the dreams God gives you.
>
> o o o o o

It has been an honor and a joy to encourage your heart on this journey. I will not leave you here with a charge to "dream big and chase your dreams." But I do urge you to "dream big . . . with God and let Him lead." Dream on with God, sweet one. It's a dance He is calling you to.

As I wrap up this ballet of words, I want you to know that dreaming with God takes practice. Even as I was writing this book, I found myself struggling with some of my own dreaming questions. I think we'll always have questions. So we just keep taking them to our Anchor. Dreaming with God takes rehearsing His truth over and over in our hearts. Dreaming with God goes against our nature and our culture, so we will stumble and slip sometimes. However, Christ has forever picked us up, and He invites us to not only walk through life but also dance through it—with Him. I still find myself running back to Him with my dreaming questions when I forget what He has taught me. Sometimes I feel like I've tripped over my dancing feet and I'm a heaping mess of tulle, mixed up with all the dreaming messages of the world. But He keeps picking me up, and He will keep picking you up too. Be encouraged that you have One who constantly watches over your beautiful journey and guides you through every step.

○ ○ ○ ○ ○

Be encouraged that you have One who constantly watches over your beautiful journey and guides you through every step.

○ ○ ○ ○ ○

I hope and pray your dreaming heart dances today as you begin dreaming with God. Dreaming with God is truly the sweetest journey.

Prayer, Scripture, and Reflection
for Your Dreaming Heart

Lord, thank You for Your call on my life to dream with You. Hold me close through this dreaming dance and give me strength to stand strong and tall when it feels like I'm going against the grain of culture. Thank You for inviting me to dream with You. All glory and praise goes to You.

_____

_____

_____

_____

_____

_____

_____

"He will not let your foot slip—he who watches over you will not slumber." Psalm 121:3

"There is a way that appears to be right, but in the end it leads to death." Proverbs 14:12

"I have come that they may have life, and have it to the full." John 10:10

"Now to him who is able to do immeasurably more than all we ask or imagine, according to his power that is at work within us, to him be glory in the church and in Christ Jesus throughout all generations, for ever and ever! Amen." Ephesians 3:20–21

"For our struggle is not against flesh and blood, but against the rulers, against the authorities, against the powers of this dark world and against the spiritual forces of evil in the heavenly realms." Ephesians 6:12

"Be alert and of sober mind. Your enemy the devil prowls around like a roaring lion looking for someone to devour." 1 Peter 5:8

_____

_____

_____

_____

1. What are some ways you can stand strong in your dreaming dance with God?

2. When have you placed your need for fulfillment in a dream rather than in God?

3. Take some time, just you and God, to reflect on your own dreaming dance.

Final Notes of Encouragement

A t the end of a ballet performance, after the curtain went down and the audience began to disperse from the theater, the hugs began. All of us dancers would hug, cheer, and squeal with delight. We had done it. The work had been worth it. "Congratulations!" "You danced beautifully!" It didn't matter that we were sweaty. It didn't matter that our feet were throbbing. We celebrated with one another before beginning the process of unwinding and leaving the theater to get a good night's sleep and gear up to do it all over again the next day.

But before we left the stage, typically our ballet mistress or artistic director would gather us around for some notes. We pulled our comfy booties over our pointe shoes, threw on sweatshirts and leg warmers, circled up, and sat down. Oh, sitting down. It was the best gift after a long evening of dancing. As we gathered around, the ballet mistress or artistic director always first offered a short congratulatory comment on the show. But soon after, it was back to our notes for the evening. They knew that tomorrow a new audience would step foot into the theater, ready for a beautiful performance, and then the curtain would go up and the dancing would begin again. So as much as our feet hurt and as exhausted as we were, we knew listening to notes would make tomorrow's performance run smoother. The notes were like little reminders, sticky notes on our dancing. They reminded us that while performing was oh-so-fun, we had to continually remember some important things to bring a beautiful performance to the audience. The ballet mistress or artistic director would notice things in the performance that were a little off or needed improvement, and this was their time to nudge us oh-so-gently toward a stronger performance.

This happened in the studio on rehearsal days as well. After a run-through of a piece, we would gather around, ready for our notes and corrections. The notes were always very specific. Often dancers were called out individually. "Hey, Sarah, make sure you watch the shape of your foot in that arabesque next time." We took in the notes, knowing that our director or ballet mistress had our best in mind. Some notes were short and simple. Others required more explanation.

A dancer has a million things to remember when she is dancing. Getting her limbs and feet and arms and hands and head in the right position on the right beat of the music takes notes, corrections, repetition, and tons of rehearsal. I sometimes used to cringe when I got a note because it wasn't fun to be called out in front of the whole company. But as I began to understand that my directors were trying to help me, I grew to love corrections and notes. They kept me motivated and helped me be more confident onstage when I applied them.

So on that note, I thought it would be fun to wrap up this ballet of words by sending some final notes of encouragement your way. I have loved every minute of journeying with you. Let's pause and celebrate for a moment that we have discovered the sweetest dance of dreaming with God. *Hugs!* I wish I could hug you in person. Before you go, before you run off and begin your dance, here are some final notes.

I've taken the corrections I most often received as a ballerina and turned them into little sticky notes for your heart as you step into your dreaming journey with God. Some of these may repeat things I wrote in previous chapters, but I think they are worth repeating. As a dancer, often the notes that were repeated the most grabbed my attention the most and helped me improve. Maybe this chapter can be a reference for you in the future when you have hit a rough patch in your sweetest dance. A quick guide of things to remember as you dream with God.

So let's pretend we're on the stage after a show. You've slipped your booties over your pointe shoes, thrown on a comfy sweatshirt and some leg warmers (I sense some of you have the giggles right now), and we've circled up. I've got my notepad and my pencil. Now you rest your feet, rest your heart, rest your dreaming thoughts for a bit. Sit back. Just take in some notes of encouragement, some final thoughts for your dreaming, dancing journey that I don't want you to forget.

Stand tall.

> "Listen, stay alert, stand tall in the faith, be courageous, and be strong."
>
> 1 Corinthians 16:13 (The Voice)

May we remember all the reasons that we, as God's daughters, can stand taller in our daily dances and dreaming journeys. It's so much easier to believe the world's messages to our hearts: not good enough, not pretty enough, not successful enough, not smart enough, not . . . whatever is . . . enough. But Christ invites us to stand taller in our hearts as we soak in the sweet truth that He is enough and that because of Him, we are enough. We can let go of trying to be enough and instead embrace His blessings of righteousness and love and His saving grace. Something happens when we stand a little taller in light of the truths we know about how our Savior sees us—our hearts dance and we reflect His light to a hurting world.

Stand a little taller today in your heart as you soak in the jewels of being a chosen, adopted, and loved daughter of the King.

Deepen your plié.

> "I pray that you, being rooted and established in love, may have power, together with all the Lord's holy people, to grasp how wide and long and high and deep is the love of Christ."
>
> Ephesians 3:17–18

For a ballet dancer, plié is probably *the* most important movement. Plié is simply bending the knees. It can be from two feet or from one foot. Plié is like a springboard for a dancer. The deeper the plié, the bigger a dancer can jump. The deeper the plié, the more grounded, sturdy, and steady a dancer becomes. The deeper the plié, the more control a dancer has over her limbs. Dreaming with God and dancing daily with Him through life requires a lot out of us. We are busy gals. We juggle a lot of stuff. May we remember that the key to living well is actually going deeper with Christ. You see, without that deepening in our relationship with Jesus, we become spiritually dry, physically fatigued, frazzled, worn-out, and burnt-out. Without a deep walk with Jesus, we can get so busy doing and accomplishing that our souls simply grow depleted. May we make our most precious goal to go deeper with our Savior.

Dance big.

> "Let them praise his name with dancing."
>
> Psalm 149:3

One correction that a dancer may receive quite often over the course of her dancing career is this one: "dance big!" Or oftentimes:

"dance bigger!" It can feel frustrating at times to hear that same correction over and over because there is a lot to think about—dancing precisely in step with the music, keeping lines in check, ensuring the movement is just right, and making sure the head, arms, shoulders, feet, everything are at the correct angles. A dancer is called to dance big, but often she can get so caught up in seeking perfection in her technique that she dances small.

Dancing big requires letting go—letting go of fear, insecurity, and the quest for perfection. Dancing big is this place we get to as dancers where we are so free and so enjoying the moment that big dancing spills out. The bigger we dance, the greater the dancing is. Dancing big doesn't mean we forget our quest for correct technique, but it does mean we've got to let go of some of our perfectionistic tendencies.

In this dance of life, what if we let go of our fears? What if we let go of our insecurities? What if we let go of our quests for perfection? What if we let go of worrying about who's watching or who's not watching?

How can you dance big in your life? How can you let go of whatever is weighing you down and instead praise and trust God in a big way? What if you lived your life full-out by fully trusting in the Savior of the world? Dance big through life!

Hold your core.

"Let us hold unswervingly to the hope we profess, for he who promised is faithful."

Hebrews 10:23

If a dancer lets go of her stomach muscles, she loses strength. It's so hard to hold in the abdominal muscles, to "lace them up" kind of like shoelaces through the ribs and abs area. But it's the key to strength. It's the key to beautiful lines. A dancer works day in and day out at maintaining strong abdominal muscles because a strong core gives her strength for her entire body as well as protection from injuries, specifically to her back. When a dancer's core goes loose, her body loses its energy and strength, and her dancing loses its edge. Holding the core is vital to a dancer's dancing.

In our dance of life, we can easily lose sight of Christ. We can grow burdened with our to-do lists, our doing, and our planning. And we can become bogged down with discouragement as we listen to the news or scroll through our newsfeeds. We can so easily forget to hold on to our hope.

May we dance through life differently and hold unswervingly to the faith we profess, for He who promised is faithful. We can anchor our hope in Christ. We can have the hope of Christ in our hearts every day of the year. May we remember that the most important thing we can do each day is "hold our core," or in this instance, hold on to our hope.

Daughter, where in your life do you need to hold onto your hope? Christ is your hope. He is your eternal salvation. He is your constant companion. He is your counselor. He is your never-ending hope, always. May your heart keep tuned in to Christ, holding on to Him as your perfect hope. He is your strong center. He is your strength. He is your anchor. And here's the sweet thing: He never lets go of you. He is always with you. He is always holding your hand. Hold on to Him by letting your heart fully embrace His presence in your life. Let the Savior be your core. Your center. Your everything.

Don't look down.

"Let your eyes look straight ahead; fix your gaze directly before you."

Proverbs 4:25

The problem with a dancer looking down at her feet while working at the ballet barre is this: looking down takes the whole body out of correct alignment. As she looks down, her shoulders subtly scoot one way, which results in her upper body twisting out of place slightly, which then results in the waist sinking into one hip, causing the hip to become off-center and preventing the leg from working properly from the hip socket. That twistedness then puts extra pressure on the knees and ankles. Looking down, while it feels good and comfortable for the mind, wreaks havoc on the body.

For a dancer to keep her eyes, head, and chin up and resist the temptation to check the mirror over and over takes incredible discipline. But when she sinks into that discipline, her muscles and whole body are freed up to work properly.

In the dance of life, we "look down" in many ways that twist our spiritual growth so much that we lose our footing, fail to grow, and miss out on a deeper walk with the Lord.

Looking down can be kind of an inward withdrawal from truly engaging in life because we feel not good enough, not adequate enough, or not popular enough, so we keep our focus on our own feet; we stay comfortable in our own little bubble, not wanting to cause too much of a ruckus. We stay inward, wanting to be strong and confident and a powerful vessel for the Lord, but our insecurities or fears or whatever else holds us back. Meanwhile, our looking down actually distorts how God might want to use us. We have trouble believing He has plans for us.

Maybe for you looking down is looking to the past. You may feel like your past makes you unworthy of a good future. Or maybe you, like me, look too far into your future, wondering how it all will work out. You get so focused on looking ahead that you miss out on what's happening right now.

I love this little gem from Proverbs 4:25: "Let your eyes look straight ahead; fix your gaze directly before you." What wisdom!

May we remember we have a Savior we can look up to, and we can always hold our gaze on Him. He holds His gaze on us too, all day long. When we keep our gaze on Him, we don't have to look down anymore. When we keep our gaze on Him, we're free to dance through life the way He intended—with great peace, joy, and confidence in Him. Don't look down, dear one.

Stretch your feet.

> "I bring you good news that will cause great joy for all the people."
>
> Luke 2:10

> "Come near to God and he will come near to you."
>
> James 4:8

A dancer has to really stretch her feet, as in, point them from the ankle all the way through the tips of the toe in every position. It's easy to get by with "kind of" engaging the muscles and pointing the feet, but it takes discipline to really stretch the feet. As a spectator at a ballet performance, I want to see *really* stretched feet pointing *all* the way. It's not comfortable for a dancer, but it looks so beautiful and enhances her technique.

This brings me to our dance of life. We can get by with "kind of" tuning in to God's voice. We can get by with "kind of" giving our lives to Him. But that "kind of" mentality keeps us from really experiencing Christ the way He designed us to. However, dreaming with God allows us to really tune in to our Savior.

I don't know where you are in your walk with Jesus but know that He's inviting you to stretch your heart, your faith, and your preconceived ideas about Him by drawing closer to Him and discovering everything He has for you through His Holy Spirit. Christ has more peace for you. Christ has more joy for you. Christ has more freedom for you. Christ has more hope for you. Christ has more power for you. Christ has more grace for you. Will you stretch your heart and take a step toward Him?

Warm up.

"Let the morning bring me word of your unfailing love, for I have put my trust in you. Show me the way I should go, for to you I entrust my life."

Psalm 143:8

Warming up the body before any type of exercise is important for preventing injuries. I always loved to bundle up in my favorite warm-up pants, a big, comfy sweater, leg warmers, and booties during warm-up class to keep my feet and body warm so that my muscles were ready for the ballet performance. A ballet dancer warms up to get her blood flowing so her muscles can then stretch, allowing her to jump and dance. Warming up properly is a dancer's foundation to beautiful dancing.

Sweet one, spending time with Jesus warms up our souls, hearts, and minds for the day and for life. Just as a dancer would not jump into her grande allegro without warming up, we too should not jump into our days without warming up our souls with Christ's love and presence.

During long days in the studio or at the theater, a dancer has to stay warmed up. She follows a constant cycle . . . put on warm-ups, warm up, rehearse or perform, rest a bit, put warm-ups back on, keep moving the body so it doesn't get too cold, warm up some more, rehearse or perform again. I remember one time my director nearly scolded me for walking around backstage without my full warm-up attire on. He was afraid I was going to get too cold and pull a muscle onstage. He was watching out for me by making sure I was staying warm.

In life, God doesn't say our time with Him has to look a certain way or be a certain time of day. But when we start our day with Him, He warms our souls and gears us up for the day. And then He continues warming our souls as we walk with Him throughout our day. As we look to Him for help, ask Him for wisdom, and invite Him into the details of our day, He swoops in, wraps us in His love and comfort, and keeps us warm.

The sweetest dance is about discovering the warmth of Christ for your own heart. Let Christ warm you up with His Word, His company, and His Spirit throughout your daily dance and your dreaming journey.

Rest well.

> "Truly my soul finds rest in God; my salvation comes from him."
>
> Psalm 62:1

When I was dancing full-time, the best rest for me after a weekend of performing or a day of rehearsing included putting my feet up, placing a heating pad on my back, and slipping ice packs under my calves. I had to take pressure off my red, swollen feet and help my body feel normal after intense work in pointe shoes.

Now, as a mom of three sons, the best rest for me is taking a hot bath after getting them to bed, putting my feet up (not much has changed), watching an episode of *Dancing with the Stars* or a good sitcom with my hubby, and then diving into a good book (I really only last ten minutes tops reading my book) before crashing out for a good night's sleep.

God designed us for rest, for times of nothing, for times of not feeling guilty for not accomplishing anything, for times of recharging and refueling and just being. But He also designed our souls to need a different type of rest . . . resting in Him. Resting in Him can sound like we have to do something, such as pray, read the Bible, or go to church. And those are awesome things, but really, resting in Him is more of a state of our souls that we can live from. It's a quiet strength that stems from a deep knowing that God loves us and is guiding us. We rest in Him even as we go about our busy lives. Our hearts can know rest when we know Christ. But finding that sense of rest takes time. As we curl up close to Him by spending time with Him and inviting Him into the details of our day, our souls grow restful, our hearts feel His peace, and we experience real, true soul rest. Amid the hectic pace of life, may we remember to rest well, to stop, to pause, to notice, to breathe in God's presence, gifts, and grace.

Don't look around.

> "The angel went to her and said, 'Greetings, you who
> are highly favored! The Lord is with you.'"
>
> Luke 1:28

If I regret anything about my dancing career, it's this: that I spent all that time looking around at the other dancers, wishing I were more like them. It's definitely good to study other dancers' technique and learn from them. But I wished I were more like them—and that's a whole different thing. It's funny how in professional ballet when you're a snowflake or a flower in the corps de ballet, you have to work hard to be like everyone else and to blend in. However, when you're a soloist, you get the opportunity to stand out. But dancers are so often trained to blend in that they don't know how to stand out anymore. I remember trying so hard to be like other dancers that I didn't even know what being me looked like.

I think of Mary, the mother of Jesus. God picked her out. God intentionally purposed her with a mighty calling to carry the Son of God. He had perfect plans and a holy design for her.

He does for you too. I want to encourage you that God sees you and He just wants you to be *you*. You may feel like nothing special. You may wonder what you could possibly be good at or how God could possibly use you. But know this: trying to be someone else is putting an obstacle up between you and who God designed you to be. God wants you to embrace the gift of you. God picked you out. God intentionally purposed you with a mighty calling to carry His presence into a hurting world. You can stop looking around because of Him. You can be you. You can be you because you have God in you. You carry the very presence of God because you know Jesus. And He wants to do amazing things through you. When you let Christ take over, you start becoming who He designed you to be. You, like Mary, are highly favored. The Lord is with you.

=== **Wear your jewels.** ===

> "Mary treasured up all these things and pondered them in her heart."

Luke 2:19

My ballet teacher from the studio where I grew up training as a young dancer painted a great visual picture for us regarding our posture that has always stuck with me. She would tell us to carry ourselves as if our neck were adorned with the most beautiful jewels and that the jewels were even scattered across our shoulders, down our arms, and all the way to our fingertips. I don't know where you're sitting right now, dancer or not, but just think about that for a minute. Does it make you sit up a little taller, lift your chin a bit, and even feel a bit like a princess?

I love that visual picture because it invites a dancer to carry herself in such a way that she feels confident, graceful, and strong; it makes her feel different about herself, special. It's hard to remember, though, to activate that sparkling visual when you're concentrating on the steps or trying to get through a difficult piece of choreography, but when a dancer does carry herself that way, it's breathtakingly beautiful.

We have so many jewels lavished on us as daughters of Christ, but we so easily forget all that we have in Him. So I just want to offer these jewels from Psalm 103 to remind you of all you have in Christ so that you ooze confidence, grace, and strength from the inside out:

He forgives all your sins.

He heals all your diseases, all your muck, all your stuff, all your hurts.

He redeems your life from the pit.

He crowns you with love and compassion.

He satisfies your desires with good things.

He renews you day in and day out.

You are also chosen (see 1 Pet. 2:9), adopted (see Eph. 1:5), lavished with grace (see vv. 7–8), and dearly loved (see Col. 3:12).

As you dance your dance and dream with God, may you wear all your jewels, wear all your benefits as a daughter of the King. May knowing all that you have because of Christ light up your soul for this dance of life.

Invite the audience in.

"Here I am! I stand at the door and knock."

Revelation 3:20

One thing I always tried to keep in the forefront of my mind when I was performing onstage was to invite the audience in to make sure I was making them feel like they were right there in the story of the ballet. To invite the audience in is simply to intrigue them, to welcome them, to dance for them. To invite the audience in is to fully engage with them.

In the hustle and bustle of our daily dances, we must be fully engaged. First, invite in our audience of One—Christ. May we fully open our hearts and lives to His love and presence. May we fully believe that the more we invite Him in, the more we will transform into His likeness.

May we also invite others into our dances. Who in your life can you love well this season? Who can you invite in? Who can you take time to listen to, take time to call, take time to give a special gift, take time to encourage, take time to help? Dancing without inviting the audience in is dancing with something missing. The performance doesn't feel quite right when we forget the audience. They are just as important as the dancers, the scenery, the lights, the stage makeup, the music, and all the behind-the-scenes crew. Without the audience, there is no performing. Living without inviting Christ and others into our lives is living with something missing. Something doesn't feel right when we forget our audience of One and the ones we love. He and our loved ones and neighbors are what life is all about.

Smile to the back row.

"I pray that you . . . know this love that surpasses knowledge—that you may be filled to the measure of all the fullness of God."

Ephesians 3:17, 19

"Above all else, guard your heart, for everything you do flows from it."

Proverbs 4:23

My ballet teacher growing up used to always remind us to "smile all the way to the back row." She wanted us to smile to the very last row at the very back of the theater, especially to the very last row at the very top balcony of the auditorium. The audience members sitting in that row may have been far away from the stage, but they were the ones we needed to project to. Her reminder made us project our character and stage presence in a much bigger way than if we were simply dancing for the people in the front row.

Our gaze impacts the state of our hearts. Where we gaze, where we focus, impacts what we think, how we feel, and how we live. Just as it's hard in a performance to continuously smile all the way to the back row, it's hard in real life to continuously keep our gaze in the right direction. I encourage you to keep your gaze on Christ, His good gifts, and His presence in your life.

Soak it all in—

"Be still, and know that I am God."

Psalm 46:10

"Put off your old self, which is being corrupted by its deceitful desires; to be made new in the attitude of your minds; and to put on the new self, created to be like God in true righteousness and holiness."

Ephesians 4:22–24

I was so nervous during some ballet performances that I didn't really fully enjoy the performance. I was too busy worrying about a certain step or slipping or whatever it was, I would realize later, that I missed the joy of dancing in the moment. Dancing in the moment isn't really something you can teach a ballet student. You can't convince a dancer to do it, but when they do, unfazed by nerves or fears, the most beautiful dancing takes place.

And I think about how in the dance of life, we can so easily plow through our days that sometimes we miss the beauty of living. Have you been there? Have you felt that way? I just urge all of us to pause, to be still, to stop, to pull over, to hop off the treadmill of busyness and simply soak it all in. It's not easy. It goes against everything in our nature, but here's the sweet thing: we have a new nature because of our Savior. The old nature has passed away and a new nature resides in us. Sometimes we forget. In fact, I often forget. I often need to sit down and soak all this truth in. I need to soak in that I have the Spirit of God living inside me. This truth is so miraculous, it's hard to wrap our minds around it and understand exactly what it means. But let's hold on to this: when we let our hearts get still enough to soak in God's presence, our new nature starts to take over. The Holy Spirit that resides in us has room to move and work as we get still enough to let Him take over. Life urges us to hurry because there's so much to do. Yes, there's so much to do. But the Spirit urges us in a different way to sit down with Him and soak in more of Him. How can you set aside the busyness of today and soak in more of Christ? More joy awaits you.

Pack your dance bag.

> "'Martha, Martha,' the Lord answered, 'you are worried and upset about many things, but few things are needed—or indeed only one. Mary has chosen what is better, and it will not be taken away from her.'"
>
> Luke 10:41–42

A ballet dancer's dance bag is everything to her. It holds everything she could possibly need. And without it, well, not much dancing can happen. Here's the short version of the contents of my typical daily dance bag: ballet shoes (two pairs), pointe shoes (two to five pairs), toe pads (two pairs), leg warmers, warm socks, booties, leotards (at least two), tights (at least two pairs), sweater, jacket, bandages, toe tape, blister pads, scissors, needle, thread, hairspray, hair gel, body splash, toenail clippers, IcyHot, ibuprofen, foot roller, shoe scraper, stage makeup, bobby pins, hairpins, brush, makeup remover wipes, snacks, Gatorade, phone, headphones, journal and pen (always!), a good book . . . that's just the basics. You get the idea. A ballet dancer's dance bag contains everything she could possibly need in a rehearsal, a performance, a backstage quick change, or a backstage emergency. It prepares her for anything.

In our dances through life, may we remember that time with our Savior is everything. May our time with Him rise to the very top of our priorities. But it shouldn't be simply another line to check off our to-do list or a way to prove ourselves to God or get on His "good list." No, we must understand that hanging out with Jesus is the most important thing to prepare us for life. During our time with Jesus, we gain access to all the tools, resources, preparation, and wisdom we could possibly need. He invites us to get to know Him so that He may love on us, reveal His heart to us, and transform our hearts. He's calling out to you and inviting you to come spend time with Him so He may lead you through this dance of life. He wants you to find the life He created you for. He doesn't want you to miss it . . . or miss Him. Will you choose to make Him your everything?

Dance with confidence.

"Each of you should use whatever gift you have received to serve others, as faithful stewards of God's grace in its various forms."

1 Peter 4:10

"Call to me and I will answer you and tell you great and unsearchable things you do not know."

Jeremiah 33:3

Something that breaks my heart when I'm watching a ballet class, coaching a dancer, or watching a performance is when I see a dancer who has lost her confidence. I have been that dancer, and I know what it feels like. Sometimes a dancer gets lost in the tangled web of comparison, fear, or insecurity. That's when the joy slips away and a dancer must find her way back to dance with confidence again. I sometimes want to take a dancer by the shoulders, look straight into her eyes, and give her a pep talk. "You have what it takes. You are a beautiful dancer. You have a gift. You need to believe it." When a dancer sets aside the lies she's been believing and instead focuses on the truth about herself, her confidence comes back, and she dances the most beautiful kind of dancing.

I don't know whether your confidence has slipped in life, but I want to take you by the shoulders and tell you that with God you have what it takes. You are beautiful. You have gifts. You need to believe it. I don't know specifically what your gifts are, but I pray you discover whatever God has given to you. Some of you may not know how God has gifted you. You may wonder, like I have in the past, *How can God use me?* But please know that you can call to Him, and He will delight to show you and to "tell you great and unsearchable things you do not know." Let Him fill you with the confidence you need to display your beautiful gifts. And hold on to this: when you use your gifts, you are administering God's grace to others. Call to Him. He believes in you. When you trust that He does, you will glow with confidence.

=== **Stay focused.** ===

> "Set your hearts on things above, where Christ is, seated at the right hand of God. Set your minds on things above, not on earthly things."
>
> Colossians 3:1–2

Final Notes of Encouragement

"Direct my footsteps according to your word."

Psalm 119:133

Putting on stage makeup, for me, was not just putting on fake eyelashes and having fun with bright red lipstick. Putting on stage makeup was getting in the zone. The time I spent applying eye shadow, blush, and mascara while listening to music that stirred my heart helped me get my mind focused on the performance. Sometimes I would chitchat with the dancer next to me and we would swap stories and so forth, but most times, the dancer next to me was doing the same thing . . . staying focused. Jumping onstage unfocused, unprepared mentally, can be dangerous. That time sitting in front of the dressing room mirror was the first step in preparing for a great performance. Like dancing, it takes discipline to set our hearts and our minds on Christ. It takes effort to invite Him into our days, to study His Word, and to pray. It takes choosing Him over other things.

After I finished my stage makeup, I would always head to the backstage area to slip into my pointe shoes just a few minutes before the curtain went up and the show began. I loved watching all the behind-the-scenes stuff going on—the lighting crew testing the lights, the stage crew sweeping the stage, the stage manager reviewing cues, and the other dancers going over their choreography. In our daily dances and our dreaming journeys, we can stay focused on Christ because He's doing all the behind-the-scenes stuff. He's taking care of our dreaming hearts, which have hopes, plans, desires, and dreams. He knows the details of our hearts. He knows His plans for us. He knows where He's taking us. We don't have to figure all that out. He's directing our footsteps. Our jobs? Stay focused on Him. He'll take care of everything going on behind the scenes.

Point your toes.

> "Jesus answered, 'I am the way and the truth and the life. No one comes to the Father except through me.'"
>
> John 14:6

Probably the first correction a ballet dancer will ever receive in her early training years is to point her toes. And the funny thing is, she will hear that correction over and over and over throughout her career. It can't be said enough: "point your toes." I have a "point" for you as you head out into your own dance with the Lord. I don't think you could ever hear it enough. I don't think I could say it enough. And I don't think your heart has heard it enough: God has special plans for your life. I know I've written it to you a zillion times. I know you may have skimmed over it because you've already heard it a zillion times, but I want you to take it in, really take it in. God has special plans for your life. He designed you for a purpose. He made you unique from anyone else, and He loves you more than you could possibly imagine. The way to know that plan? The way to discover who He wants you to be? He is the way. He is the way, the truth, and the life. Eternally, yes! That would have been enough of a gift. But it's true on earth too. He wants to lead you through this dance of life. I used to hear people say, "God has a special plan for your life," and I always thought that was just so cool. I wanted to discover it because it sounded exciting and adventurous. Of course, it is, but what's sweeter is that discovering God's special plans for our lives is really about more than journeying through life with Jesus and growing dependent on Him for direction, wisdom, and love. It's intimately knowing Jesus and walking with Him; there's no greater thing. So point your toes if you're dancing, but more important, remember God has special plans for your life.

Stay hydrated.

"My soul thirsts for you."

Psalm 63:1 ESV

"Whoever drinks the water I give them will never thirst. Indeed, the water I give them will become in them a spring of water welling up to eternal life."

John 4:14

"Whoever believes in me, as Scripture has said, rivers of living water will flow from within them."

John 7:38

For a ballet dancer, an athlete, a mom, a gal, any person, staying hydrated is incredibly important. Keeping that constant source of water nearby is key to functioning at our best. I have a bit of a tendency to hydrate more on coffee than water, especially when I'm writing, so I have to be really careful to make sure my water intake outweighs my coffee intake. But I also want to talk about a different kind of hydrating. Our souls need Living Water. Our souls thirst for a deep connection to our Savior. Our souls were designed to function best on a constant source, a constant flow of Living Water.

I can sense when I need to get with my Savior. My soul feels thirsty. My tendency is to try to quench that thirst with something else. But I have found that Jesus is the only thing that truly quenches my deep soul thirst. In your day-to-day dances and in your giant leaps toward the dreams God is dancing with you, take time every day to hydrate your soul with Christ's Living Water. God came down to earth, born in the manger, to quench your thirsty soul. Notice when your soul feels thirsty. Notice when you feel that soul unrest, that void, that nudge that something feels off. That's how God designed you. That ache is your soul needing to connect with your Savior. When you feel that, run to Him. Grab your Bible. Grab your journal. Grab some coffee. Find a cozy nook. Sit with Him. Let Him hydrate your soul. I can't really say how He will quench your thirst. He does it in ways unique to each person. His Word satisfies. His presence satisfies. His personal involvement in your life satisfies. His nearness satisfies. As you set about your dreaming journey, stay hydrated in Him.

Use hair gel.
(I promise this is applicable to your life!)

"Make it your ambition to lead a quiet life."

1 Thessalonians 4:11

One of the most important rules during my dancing days growing up was to use hair gel on performance days. I know it sounds very insignificant compared to other things, but it was key. We were trained to use serious gel. We used to use the brand called Dippity-do. First, we would wet our hair, then we would take a brush (the kind that wouldn't make "railroad tracks" in our hair), smooth our hair into a tight ponytail, and then secure it with a hair rubber band. Then we would get a big scoop of Dippity-do and slather it all over our hair before repeating the hairbrush strokes to smooth out all the hair wispies. Wispies are loose hairs, and the reason ballet dancers don't like wispies is that from stage, they show! Under the stage lights, hair wispies seem to glow and take on a character all their own. And that's a no-no. They look sloppy, and a dancer doesn't want sloppy hair onstage. After applying the gel, we would then spray hairspray all over our heads. Later, after the show, our hair was literally crispy, but it looked beautiful when we were dancing onstage. I carried this hair gel routine into my professional dancing years because I discovered that onstage, slicked-back, smooth, no-wispy hair was professional. Wispies are distracting. Smoothing back all those loose strands simplifies things.

I promised you this was going to apply to your life, so here we go! Simplifying our lives actually beautifies them. What's distracting you? What's frazzling you? How can you simplify your life? Sometimes we take on too much. Sometimes we try to do it all. Sometimes we get so lost in our doing that we forget about our living. Sometimes we live so distracted that we feel frazzled on the inside. Simplifying sorts us out. For me, simplifying means several things.

Unplugging—when I unplug from the internet, social media, and email, my soul seems to take a deep breath. As I go dark, my soul lights up.

Slowing down—when I'm aware of my pace, when I notice my rushing tendency and physically slow down my pace, my soul seems to unwind.

Saying no—when I let go of the pressure to say yes to everything and instead pray about each commitment and ask for God's wisdom, my soul seems to relax.

These are just some of the ways I simplify my life. We all feel it when our souls are growing frazzled. We all feel it when our hearts are feeling stressed. But when we simplify, we do this: "Make it [our] ambition to lead a quiet life." A quiet life of Jesus leading our hearts. It's good for the soul.

Enjoy the moments.

"Walk in the light, as he is in the light."

1 John 1:7

"'For I know the plans I have for you,' declares the LORD, 'plans to prosper you and not to harm you, plans to give you hope and a future.'"

Jeremiah 29:11

I spent many moments of my dancing career trying to figure out future moments and the next steps in my dancing career. I spent many moments wondering how dancing and being a mom was going to work. I spent many moments worrying about what life after a dancing career would look like. I spent many moments worrying about the future or dwelling over the past, and meanwhile, I was missing the present. Don't we all sometimes forget to enjoy the present? *But God is in the present moment.* God is not in the past. He was when you were there at the time, but no, He's not there now. God's not in the future either. He knows all about it and He sees it all and He will be there when you get there, but no, He's not there now. God is in the present moment, with you, dear one. Jesus came to earth to walk with you through these moments. And when we stay with Him, our hearts dance. Our hearts light up when we walk in the light as He is in the light. When we stay with Him in the moment, it's as if our hearts are proclaiming, "God has my future . . . it's in His hands." Sisters, I'm not saying this is an easy thing to do. It goes against everything in us. But I hold on to this: "For nothing will be impossible with God" (Luke 1:37 ESV). Staying present in the moment with God is possible . . . and enjoying those present moments is the most beautiful place to be.

Soak your feet.

> "I pray that you, being rooted and established in love, may have power, together with all the Lord's holy people, to grasp how wide and long and high and deep is the love of Christ."
>
> Ephesians 3:17–18

> "For the word of God is alive and active."
>
> Hebrews 4:12

A dancer has to take care of her feet. The best remedy for aching, red, raw, sore, and tired feet is to soak them. A bucket of ice-cold water revives and renews the muscles for the next day of dancing. As the icy cold surrounds the muscles, the feet start to heal. Just as a dancer must take good care of her feet because they carry her in her dancing, we too must take care of what carries us through our dreaming dances—our hearts.

I pray you have felt your heart start to soak in the goodness of God's love. I pray you have begun to feel Christ's love wrapping around your heart and starting to revive, renew, and repair it. I pray your heart is starting to come alive as you soak in the good news of our Savior. I want to encourage you to keep soaking in the steadying power of God's Word. Keep your heart grounded in Scripture. The way to keep your heart rooted in Christ is to keep your heart and mind in His Word. His Word is everything. It supports you in your dreaming journey, guiding and encouraging you. God's Word is powerful, active, and alive. God's Word is your secure footing. God's Word lights up your heart. God's Word is your steady foundation. Take care to get your heart in God's Word. God wants to use it to speak truth to you. He wants to wash your heart in His truth and pour His truth into your soul.

Trust your partner.

> "For I am the LORD your God who takes hold of your
> right hand and says to you, Do not fear; I will help
> you."
>
> Isaiah 41:13

I love dancing with a partner onstage. When a male dancer holds a ballerina just right on her leg, lifts her high into the air, and carries her across the stage effortlessly, it makes my heart dance! The ballerina must completely trust her partner. And sometimes it's really hard. Sometimes a ballerina wants to take the lead. She wants to be in control. But she has to trust. She has to let the male dancer lead. She has to trust he knows where she needs to be, when she needs to be there. She has to trust he knows what he is doing. When she does, beauty happens. The same thing is true in this dance of life. We have the best dance partner—God. When we let the Lord lead our lives, beauty happens. But it's hard to trust Him sometimes, isn't it? It's hard to truly give our lives over to Him completely. Sometimes we want to be in control, to lead our own lives. We think we know best. But we must remember, He knows where we need to be. He knows when we need to be there. He knows what He's doing. Our lives work best when Jesus is leading. When we let Him lead, we can find a deeper joy than we've ever known before. Will you trust your Partner, your Savior?

Secure your pointe shoe ribbons.

"You will be secure, because there is hope; you will look about you and take your rest in safety."

Job 11:18

This is my greatest advice to a ballet dancer on performance day: "Secure your pointe shoe ribbons." It was also my greatest secret weapon for a successful show. By secure, I mean sew the ribbons together at the knot with a needle and thread. I usually did three or four secure knots. Then I sprayed the knots with a good dose of hairspray. Every single time. Every single performance. Because when we don't secure our pointe shoe ribbons, they can easily come undone. The worst thing ever for a ballet dancer is to be dancing beautifully onstage only to have her ribbons come undone. It's an invitation to fall. It's a distraction for the dancer. What I love about securing my pointe shoe ribbons is that once I tie that final knot and clip off the extra thread with my scissors, I know my pointe shoe ribbons are one less thing I have to worry about onstage. I don't have to wonder if they are coming undone. I can enjoy the performance fully knowing they are secured.

Daughter of Christ, as you begin your dreaming dance, you can know you're secure in Christ. You can know He's got you. You can know He loves you. You can know you will spend eternity in heaven with Him if you believe He died on the cross for your sins and rose again for you. On top of all that, you can know He wants to dance with you through life, leading you, guiding you, and helping you. You can rest assured you're His daughter. You can rest assured He's watching over your sweetest dance. You can be fully confident He has your every step. Let your heart dance securely as you step into dreaming with God.

Dance on, sweet one. He's got you. Dreaming with God will be the sweetest dance.

Acknowledgments

First of all, I must thank Jesus. Jesus, You saw and heard and sensed and stirred and led and gathered me all along my dancing journey to this place. You brought me here. This book is a little gift I want to give to You because You brought the words, You brought the lessons, You met me in my questions along the way, and You set me on this dreaming path. I'm so grateful to You for Your constant invitation to dance with You through life. I love dancing with You.

To Brian, my husband and best friend, for believing in me from the very first time I spoke up about this little book dream. Thank you for supporting my dreams on the stage through my dancing years, through motherhood, and now typing these words. I love dancing through life with you. Thank you for helping me through all the tedious parts of this book and encouraging me in so many ways through your pep talks and prayers. Being married to you is the best part of all of it.

To Camp, Cooper, and Colt, my three precious boys. You guys make my day every day. Your precious hearts are the sweetness God knew I needed. Thank you for supporting Mommy in her author dreams. Thank you for teaching me what it looks like to live in the moment, to laugh and play, and to be confident in who God made us to be. Thank you for listening when I ramble off book ideas, for smiling and giving me a thumbs-up. I pray you always dream with God leading the way. I know you know He has adventures just for you. I love being your mommy. God uses you guys all the time to spur me on, encourage me, and bless me. You are my superheroes.

To Mom, you taught me to dream with God. Thank you for pointing me to Christ all along my journey, ever so gently, ever so sweetly. Thank you for praying this baby into fruition and praying for my dancing heart all these years. I could have told a hundred stories of how you have encouraged my dreaming heart through the years. Your treasures of encouragement and truth are laced through all the pages. I'm so blessed by you.

To Dad, thank you for always being so supportive of my endeavors. For saying yes when I wanted to dance professionally, for your endless support and love and encouragement for me as a mom, and for your sweetness and excitement regarding my writing. You're the best.

To Granny, thank you for encouraging me in my writing and my dancing all this time. It means the world to me. I love you dearly.

To Katie Norris, my sweet sister. When I blurted out two heart desires years ago in a restaurant in Canton, Texas—a leotard line and a devotional book—you gave me a heaping scoop of encouragement that I could write. (Maybe we will tackle the leotard line later.) The Lord has used your dreaming heart time after time after time to inspire and bless me with encouragement. You're one special sister. Thank you for talking through book ideas with me while we get our toes done and drink our coffee. Thank you for our fun photo sessions and for the beautiful photos for my website. Seeing you walk in the dreams God has for you, your joy and the light that you are, simply blesses my soul. And seeing you with Rose is a constant reminder that dreaming with God really is the sweetest dance.

To Reece Norris, I can't figure out how to say thank you enough for taking such time, energy, and effort to support my writing dream. Not only that, you have encouraged me that God's timing, plans, and ways are perfect. I'm incredibly blessed to get to work with you. Thank you, Reece.

To Ben, Jenn, Kyle, and Mel, you have been so supportive. You have listened to my ideas, prayed for me, and brainstormed with me. You have encouraged me more than you know. I love each of you dearly; thank you for cheering me on.

To my entire, huge, big, humongous family on both sides . . . each and every one of you . . . thank you for your encouragement and support. Our family blesses my life so much.

To sweet, precious friends who have prayed for me and encouraged me along this journey (you know who you are), thank you. Thank you for the phone calls, hugs in the Target aisles, texts and notes of encouragement, and for talking writing with me when I run into you on my walks. Your little bursts of encouragement are heaven-sent.

To my blog readers and sweet friends on social media, thank you for reading my devotionals and words. Your comments and presence have truly blessed me. Encouraging you in your journey with the Lord is such a joy for me, but what you may not realize is that you have encouraged me. I wish I could hand a book to you in person and give you a hug. I hope I get to meet some of you.

To the dancing hearts who I had the honor of journeying through my dancing years with, Brent and Judy Klopfenstein, Stephen Mills, Michelle Martin, Truman Finney, Paul Mejia, Alexander Vetrov, and many precious friends, I'm so grateful for your influence, mentorship, and belief in my dancing.

To Dan Balow and the Steve Laube Agency, without you, this book wouldn't be happening. I'm beyond honored to get to work with you. You've been a vital part of my dreaming journey, and I'm incredibly thankful. Dan, thank you for believing in me and for all the behind-the-scenes work you've done on my behalf to find a place for my words. Thank you for answering all of my questions along the way and for your kindness and willingness to guide me through this journey. I feel like I found not only an agent but also a mentor for this writing and publishing journey.

To Rebekah Guzman and the Baker Books team, I cannot thank you enough for this opportunity. Thank you for dreaming with me and believing in me. Rebekah, thank you times a million for saying yes.

To Nicci Jordan Hubert, my editor, thank you for taking my ballet of words and pointing the way to a clearer message. I appreciate you encouraging me through this process by showing me that it's much like the rehearsal process in ballet. Thank you for helping me polish and refine this concoction of words from my heart.

To Amy Ballor, my project editor, thank you for your expertise and careful review of my manuscript in its final stages. I learned so much through the process, and I am in your debt for helping me polish my words.

To Patti Brinks, Twila Bennett, and the rest of the team who created my book cover, I truly cannot thank you enough for so tenderly creating a cover that reflected me and my message so perfectly. I wish I could hug you!

To Erin Smith and Erin Bartels, thank you for your gracious help and guidance on the marketing side of things and for so kindly answering all my questions.

To you, dear reader, I have been thinking about you, wondering who you are and how you are. Mom and I truly believe books jump off of bookshelves and land in our hands exactly when we need them, so I want you to know how grateful I am that this book caught your eye. I am praying for you that your heart will feel God's love toward you as you read. Thank you, sincerely, from my whole heart, for picking up this book.

Glossary of Ballet Terms

ballet positions. In classical ballet, there are five positions of the feet. Every step a ballet dancer makes comes from these basic positions. In each position, the toes and knees are turned out.

- *first position.* Heels are together.
- *second position.* Feet are shoulder-width apart.
- *third position.* One foot is in front of the other with the heel of one foot touching the inside of the other foot.
- *fourth position.* Similar to third position but in a crossed position with space between the feet.
- *fifth position.* Feet are in a crossed position with no space between the feet; the toe of the front foot touches the heel of the back foot

dégagé. An exercise at the barre where a dancer brushes the foot off the floor into a low position with a fully stretched foot to the front, side, or back. Dégagés are typically quick, sharp exercises executed at a quick tempo. They are excellent for warming up the leg muscles and are also the beginning preparations for big jumps later in a ballet class.

pas de deux. A dance for two. A pas de deux involves intricate partnering skills, lifts, and turns that a male and female dancer perform together.

piqué arabesque. Stepping directly onto the point or demi-point (half point) of the working leg and lifting the back leg to a ninety-degree angle.

pirouette. A fully executed turn on one leg.

plié. A bending of the knees. A ballet dancer typically begins barre exercises with pliés from first, second, fourth, and fifth position and then uses plié to execute numerous other steps, jumps, and movements in the center.

rond de jambe. A circular movement of the working leg executed at the barre or in the center. Standing on one leg, the dancer circles the leg in either a clockwise or counterclockwise position.

tendues. An exercise at the barre where the dancer extends the foot to a fully stretched position, keeping the tips of the toes on the floor without putting weight into the toes. Tendues can be executed from first and fifth position to the front, side, and back at a slow or quick tempo.

About the Author

Sarah Beth Marr is a wife, mother, writer, speaker, and ballerina. Sarah danced professionally for more than fifteen years for Ballet Austin and Mejia Ballet International, formally known as Ballet Arlington. She writes at www.sarahbethmarr.com and speaks to MOPS (Mothers of Preschoolers) groups and at women's events in North Texas. She and her husband, Brian, live in Dallas, Texas, with their three sons, Camp, Cooper, and Colt.

Connect with
Sarah!

I would love to hear from you and hear about your own dreaming journey with the Lord. Please connect with me on my website or send me your story at **dreamingwithgod@sarahbethmarr.com.**

sarahbethmarr.com

SarahBethMarr

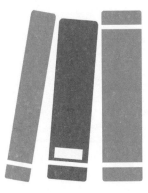

LIKE THIS
BOOK?
Consider sharing it with others!

- Share or mention the book on your social media platforms. Use the hashtag **#DreamingWithGodBook**.

- Write a book review on your blog or on a retailer site.

- Pick up a copy for friends, family, or anyone who you think would enjoy and be challenged by its message.

- Share this message on Twitter, Instagram, or Facebook: **"I loved #DreamingWithGodBook by @SarahBethMarr // @ReadBakerBooks"**

- Recommend this book for your church, workplace, book club, or class.

- Follow Baker Books on social media and tell us what you like.

 Facebook.com/ReadBakerBooks

@ReadBakerBooks